To my friend Jack,

Bob

Searching The Scriptures

As In Acts 17:11

By Robert F. Blair

First Edition – September 2014

ISBN
978-1-4602-3949-0 (Hardcover)
978-1-4602-3950-6 (Paperback)
978-1-4602-3951-3 (eBook)

These were more noble than those in Thessalonica, in that they searched the scriptures daily, whether those things were so. Acts 17:11

Produced by:

FriesenPress
Suite 300 – 990 Fort Street
Victoria, BC, Canada V8V 3K2

www.friesenpress.com

Distributed to the trade by The Ingram Book Company

Table of Contents

ACKNOWLEDGEMENTS

I am grateful for the constant encouragement and support of my sister, Ella McKellar. I am also grateful to my daughter and son-in-law, Charlotte and David Curtis and my friend Norman White, for taking the time and effort to review the material for me. Also to my friend Jane Ross for her timely advice about printing. I am grateful to my friends and neighbors, Evelyn Long and Lynne Cummings and Deanna Margil for their technical expertise. Thanks also goes to Aliesha and Marty Adsett for suggested changes to the format and to Sharon Schwartz for hours of proofreading scripture references, editing and typing every article in preparation for the publisher. I am very grateful to FriesenPress and especially the Account Manager and the Editor, for their diligence, patience and guidance in helping me to complete this project.

MESSAGE FROM THE AUTHOR

I was born in Alberta, Canada and have lived here all my life. I spent two years in the Canadian Air Force. In 1946, I married Stella Coad. We acquired land that we developed into a ranch where we raised seven children. We sold the ranch in 1998 and retired to Camrose, Alberta in 1999. Stella passed away in 2007 in her 85th year.

As a child, I was reminded that I was a sinner and that the wages of sin is death. I was also taught that God had made a way for repentant sinners to be forgiven.

> *All have sinned and come short of the glory of God.* (Romans 3:23)

> *For the wages of sin is death but the gift of God is eternal life through Jesus Christ our Lord.* (Romans 6:23)

> *The Lord is not slack concerning his promise but is longsuffering to us - ward not willing that any should perish, but that all should come to repentance.* (2 Peter 3:9)

> *Thus it is written and thus it behooved Christ to suffer, and to rise from the dead the third day: and that repentance and remission of sins should be preached in his name among all nations, beginning at Jerusalem.* (Luke 24:46-47)

I believed what I was taught, and with the assurance found in the Gospel of John and other scriptures, I have stood on those promises ever since. Some of them are as follows:

> *For God so loved the world, that he gave his only begotten Son, that whosoever believeth in him should not perish, but have everlasting life.* (John 3:16)

And as Moses lifted up the serpent in the wilderness, even so must the Son of man be lifted up: that whosoever believeth in him should not perish, but have eternal life. (John 3:14-15)

He that believeth on the Son hath everlasting life: and he that believeth not the Son shall not see life; but the wrath of God abideth on Him. (John 3:36)

Verily, verily, I say unto you, He that heareth my word, and believeth on him that sent me, hath everlasting life, and shall not come into condemnation; but is passed from death unto life. (John 5:24)

Neither is there salvation in any other: for there is none other name under heaven given among men, whereby we must be saved. (Acts 4:12)

Be it known unto you therefore, men and brethren, that through this man is preached unto you the forgiveness of sins: and by him all that believe are justified from all things, from which ye could not be justified by the law of Moses. (Acts 13:38-39)

[Paul wrote] *I kept back nothing that was profitable unto you, but have showed you, and have taught you publicly, and from house to house, testifying both to the Jews, and also to the Greeks, repentance toward God, and faith toward our Lord Jesus Christ.* (Acts 20:20-21)

That if thou shalt confess with thy mouth the Lord Jesus, and shalt believe in thine heart that God hath raised him from the dead, thou shalt be saved. For with the heart man believeth unto righteousness; and with the mouth confession is made unto salvation. (Romans 10:9-10)

For whosoever shall call upon the name of the Lord shall be saved. (Romans 10:13)

For by grace are ye saved through faith; and that not of yourselves; it is the gift of God; not of works, lest any man should boast. (Ephesians 2:8-9)

Now he which stablisheth us with you in Christ, and hath anointed us, is God; who hath also sealed us, and given the earnest [guarantee] *of the Spirit in our hearts.* (2 Corinthians 1:21-22)

Now he that hath wrought us for the selfsame thing is God, who also hath given unto us the earnest [guarantee] *of the Spirit.* (2 Corinthians 5:5)

In whom ye also trusted, after that ye heard the word of truth, the gospel of your salvation: in whom also after that ye believed, ye were sealed with that Holy Spirit of promise, which is the earnest [guarantee] *of our inheritance until the redemption of the purchased possession, unto the praise of his glory.* (Ephesians 1:13-14)

And grieve not the Holy Spirit of God, whereby ye are sealed unto the day of redemption. (Ephesians 4:30)

– Robert Blair

A paraphrase of (1 Corinthians 15: 1-4) says—This is the gospel we preach, by which those who believe are saved. That Christ died for our sins and was buried and rose again the third day according to the scriptures.

These things I have written unto you that believe on the name of the Son of God; that you may know you have otornal life—(1 John 5.13)

INTRODUCTION

Some church leaders today are expressing concern that there is not a significant difference between the behaviour and attitudes of Christians and non-Christians. I note that this was true in the church in Corinth where Christians were openly living after the flesh. In many churches today, it is the same. We are being told that the percentage of HIV-positive people in the church is no different than in the secular world.

I am convinced that assuring those who are born again that they belong to God and can never be lost (as stated in the Bible – see the last four verses in the Message from the Author) and at the same time assuring them that they can never be punished for sin they refuse to repent of (which is not stated in the Bible) is a major factor in the behaviour of the carnal Christian.

This waters down the Judgment Seat of Christ and teaches that a "bad deed" is not a moral wrong, that "terror" does not mean to terrify, and that "fear" does not mean to be afraid. And turning the Judgment Seat of Christ into a "reward" seat to make it compatible with the belief that God cannot punish His people is an outright contradiction of Hebrews 10:23-31. The God ordained punishment for willful sin is found in both Testaments. Some examples are: (Numbers 12; Miriam) (Nu 14:29–30, Men of war) (Nu 15:30–36, man who gathered sticks) (Nu 20:12, 24, Aaron) (Nu 27:12–14, Moses) (Acts 5; Ananias and Sapphira) (1 Tim 5:24–sooner or later) The righteousness of Christ has been imputed to all saints (Ro 4:22–24) So the Father does not Judge them (Jn 5:22) But the Son will do it (Jn 5:27) (2 Co 5:10–11) When He comes to receive His kingdom (Mt 19:27–30)

In an attempt to establish some credibility for myself, and to convince the reader that Theologians are not infallible in their diligence. I have listed 30 traditions that have been widely endorsed for centuries as being biblical, that cannot be found in the Bible. The first 11 are as follows:

- Noah took 120 years to build the ark. *Page 6*
- Noah was a preacher of righteousness for 120 years. *Page 7*
- Abram was older than Lot. *Page 45*
- Lot was a greedy and selfish young man. *Page 46*
- The Amalekites descended from Esau. *Page 7*
- Joseph was the eleventh son of Jacob. *Page 10*
- Joseph was sold when he was 17 years old. *Page 8*
- The 144,000 Jews who were sealed were evangelists. *Page 7*
- From Friday evening to before daylight on Sunday is equal to three days and three nights. *Page 66*
- God forgives unconditionally and commands us to do the same. *Page 50, 71*
- God cannot punish His people. *Page 58, 76*

It is my hope to show from scripture, that none of the above traditions are true and that the last three are outright contradictions of the plain teaching of the word of God. Some have said, "How can we believe that an ordinary man with no biblical training is right and all the people with degrees in theology have been wrong for hundreds of years?"

The theologians are not wrong because of any lack of intelligence on their part. They are wrong because of a lack of diligence, in searching the scriptures to see if these things are so (Acts 17: 11) Eleven of the thirty traditions in this book that I question are listed on this page as evidence of the validity of my claim. For example - (Genesis 37: 2) does not say that Joseph was sold when he was 17.

CHAPTER ONE

Ten Widely Accepted Traditions that Do Not Square with the Scriptures

It is hard to imagine that the Fathers of nearly all Christian denominations could make the same interpretive errors that have become church traditions that have endured for many generations and centuries. Yet that seems to be what has happened; presumably because no one has earnestly "searched the Scriptures to see if these things are so." I hope this book will help to change many of these misconceptions.

Sometimes people ask me how I came to be as scripturally knowledgeable as I seem to be.

It was the (Plymouth) Brethren that brought the gospel into our district and introduced us to the Bible. They emphasized searching the scriptures to see if these things were so. I was impressed with the way they could give the scripture reference for whatever claims they were making. Also about that time, there were many evangelical ministers broadcasting on the radio. We listened to Charles Fuller, J.D. Carlson, Cyril Hutchinson, William Aberhart, L.E. Maxwell, Oscar Lowery (who encouraged scripture memorization that we took part in), C.A. Sawtell, *The Lutheran Hour*, *The Hour of Decision*, and Theodore Epp. All these and more had a positive influence on my thinking. However I believe that *Hurlbut's Story of the Bible* did more to spike my interest in searching the scriptures than any other factor.

When I married Stella, we read a chapter from the Bible each day. But we found that long lists of genealogies and names we could not pronounce were pretty dry reading, so we switched to reading one story a day from *Hurlbut's Story of the Bible*. Later on we learned that it was not always accurate, but it gave us a good overview of what I call the big picture and by the time we finished it we were ready and looking forward to reviewing these stories as they were written in the Bible.

Many good books are sometimes hard to get interested in until one gets to know the characters. Hurlbut had introduced us to the characters, and the Bible took on a new life for us. Instead of just reading the words, we began to read them to see what they were saying.

Were Noah's three daughters-in-law all barren for 120 years? If Shem was only 100 years old two years after the flood, he could not have been born when Noah started to build the ark. How could that be? Just a few minutes of reading could turn into hours of research. We did not have many chores to do, and the evenings were long during the winters.

If Japheth was the oldest and Ham was the youngest, why does it always say "Shem, Ham, and Japheth"? More research. If Haran was born when Terah was 70, and Abram was born when Terah was 130, Haran would have been 60 years older than Abram. Why does Genesis 15:26 say, "Terah begat Abram, Nahor, and Haran"? More research. Haran's son Lot, whose sister married Haran's brother Nahor, must have been older than Abram even though he was Abram's nephew… more research. If Haran was 60 years older than Abram in light of the record of Genesis 10:10-25, it is easy to see how Milcah's granddaughter could be just the right age to be a bride for Isaac.

It is equally easy to see how Levi, who lived to be 137 and begat Kohath before he was 43, could have had a daughter when he was 80. This daughter would have been younger than Kohath's son Amram, whom she married even though she was Amram's aunt.

The authors of my Bible dictionary should have consulted the man who wrote " I'm my own grandpa" before they concluded that Jochebed could not have been Amram's wife (see Exodus 6:20).

Likewise, if God made a covenant with Abram when he was in Mesopotamia before he dwelt in Haran, 430 years before the Israelites left Egypt (Acts 7:2; Galations 3:17), how did the translators of Exodus 12:41 determine that the Israelites had been in Egypt for 430 years? And how do they explain how the four generations of Genesis 15:16 (consisting of Levi, Kohath, Amram, and Moses, who led them out when he was 80) add up to 430 years?

I agree with Charles Fuller that the Bible is the best commentary on the Bible and along with that the most useful book is *Strong's Concordance.*

The following is an exploration of **ten** widely accepted traditions that do not square with the scripture.

Tradition #1: Noah took 120 years to build the Ark.

Were Noah's daughters-in-law all barren for 120 years? Was God really talking to Noah when he said in Genesis 6:3 "yet his days shall be one hundred and twenty years"? It doesn't say that he was. He could have been just saying it to Himself or to other members of the Godhead, or to other angelic beings. We read that kind of language in Genesis 1:3, where "God said, 'Let there be light'", in verse 6, where "God said, 'Let there be a firmament'", and in verse 11, where "God said, 'Let the earth bring forth grass.'"

In Genesis 6:13-18, we know he was talking to Noah, and that at that point, Noah had three married sons. We also know that Noah did not have any sons until he was 500 (Genesis 5:32), one hundred years before the flood (Genesis 7:6).

Could Genesis 5:32 mean that by the time Noah was 500, he already had three sons? It could, but Genesis 11:10 tells us that, "Shem was a hundred years old, and begat Arphaxad two years after the flood." Therefore, Noah would have been 502 when Shem was born. In Hebrews 11:7, we are told that Noah believed God and moved with fear, prepared the ark. Whereas his sons were all married at that time, Noah could easily have been 590 or more. I believe he would have sold his assets that he knew were going to perish and hired skilled crews of craftsmen with hundreds of years experience (iron had been in use for over 500 years as per Genesis 4:22), who could have built the ark in a matter of months. He surely would not need 120 years to do it.

In any case, there is no scripture that says Noah took 120 years to build the ark or that he preached 120 years (2 Peter 2:5).

Tradition # 2: The Amalekites descended from Esau because Esau had a grandson named Amalek.

I have a great grandson named Micah, does that make me an ancestor of the prophet Micah? According to Numbers 24:20, "Amalek was the first of the nations." From Genesis 14:7, we learn that the Amalekites dwelt at Kadesh in the days of Abraham, at least 100 years before Esau had a grandson.

Tradition # 3: The 144,000 are evangelists and will preach the Gospel to the whole world during the tribulation.

According to Revelation 6:9 and 10, multitudes have been beheaded for their faith during the fifth seal. They would have heard the gospel from the two witnesses who prophesied for the first 1,260 days of the tribulation. (Revelation 11:3-12)

During the time of the sixth seal until Armageddon, an angel from Heaven will preach the gospel to all the world. (Revelation 14:6) It is not until sometime after the sixth seal that the 144,000 are sealed and redeemed from the earth. (Revelation 7:1-4 and 14:1-5) That would not leave much time for them to be evangelists, nor is there any Scripture that says, or even hints, that they were.

Tradition #4: Joseph was sold when he was seventeen.

According to Genesis 37: 2; "Joseph being seventeen years old, was feeding the flock with his brethren: and the lad was feeding the flock with the sons of Bilhah, and with the sons of Zilpah, his father's wives: and Joseph brought unto his father their evil report." It is obvious that he was not sold that day.

Some time after that, he told the family about his first dream, and some time after that again, he told them about his second dream. Note that they were still at Shechem because all the family were together. After Simeon and Levi murdered the men of Shalem, Jacob, Leah, Rachel, and Joseph moved to Bethel. Sometime after that as Jacob, Leah, Rachel, and Joseph were moving farther south to Ephrath, Rachel died in childbirth. The baby survived and is called Benjamin (Genesis 35:16-20). Again later, Jacob, Leah, Joseph, and Benjamin moved beyond the Tower of Edar to the vale of Hebron.

Some time after that Jacob sent Joseph to Shechem to see how his brothers were doing. How do we know they were in Hebron at this time? According to Genesis 37:14, Jacob "said to him, 'Go, I pray thee, see whether it be well with thy brethren, and well with the flocks; and bring me word again.' So he sent him out of the vale of Hebron and he came to Shechem." From there, he went on to Dothan where they sold him.

He could easily have been twenty by that time. In any case, it is pretty certain that he was not sold when he was 17. And it is for sure that there is no verse that says he was sold when he was seventeen.

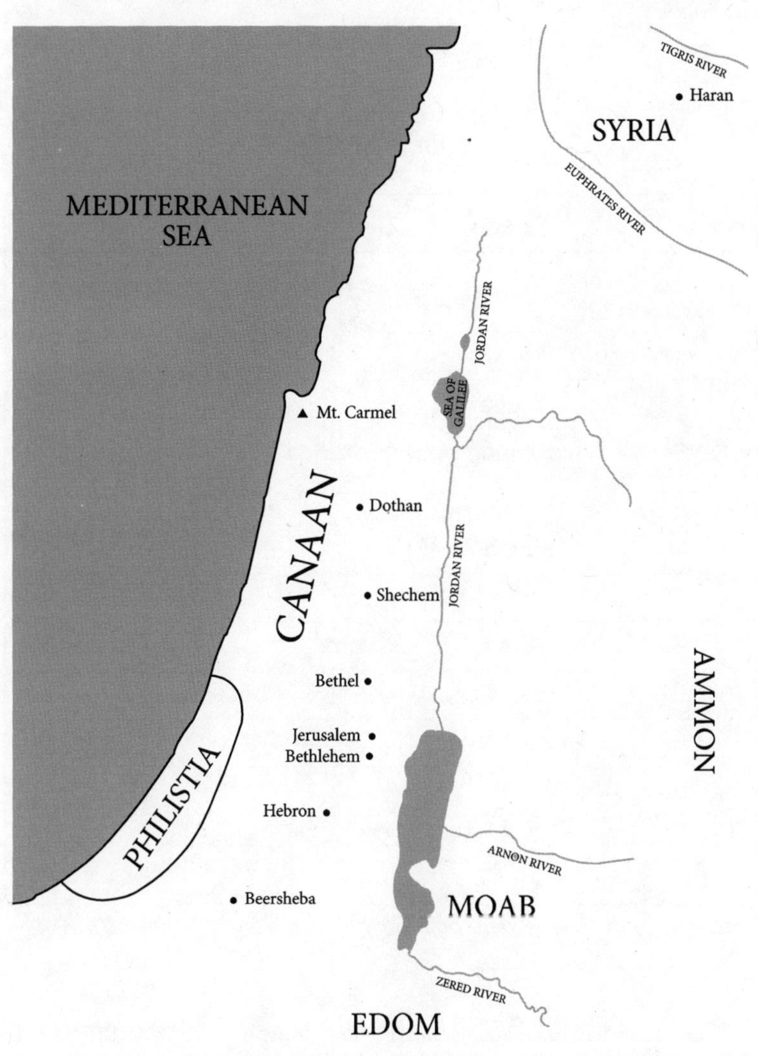

Map Of Joseph's Day

Tradition #5: Joseph was the eleventh son of Jacob.

Genesis 41:46, Genesis 45:6, and Genesis 47:8-9, tell us that when Joseph was 39, Jacob was 130.

The Sons of Jacob
(Genesis 35:22-26)

Age of Jacob	Leah	Zilpah	Rachel	Bilhah
77 Came to Haran				
84 - Married				
85	Reuben			
86	Simeon			
87	Levi			
88	Judah			
89		Gad		Dan
90		Ashur		Naphtali
91	Issachar		Joseph	
92	Zebulon			
93	Dinah			
109 - estimate			Benjamin	
147 - Died				

Issachar and Joseph were born on the same year. (Genesis 30:14-26)

This tells us that Jacob was 91 when Joseph was born. This is the basis for the rest of the chart whereby we learn that Jacob was 77 when he came to Haran and 84 when he got married. It also shows that Joseph and Issachar were born the same year (compare Genesis 30:14-26), and that Zebulun was the eleventh son, and Joseph had to be the tenth son.

Tradition # 6: Jacob stole the birthright, and many say he was so crooked he could hide behind a spiral staircase. Others say he was a thief all his life.

The Bible says: "And Esau said to Jacob, 'Feed me, I pray thee, with that same red pottage for I am faint: therefore was his name called Edom. And Jacob said, 'Sell me this day thy birthright.' And Esau said, 'Behold I am at the point to die; and what profit shall this birthright do to me?' And Jacob said, 'Swear to me this day'; and he sware unto him: and he sold his birthright to Jacob… thus Esau despised his birthright." (Genesis 25:30-34 b)

Hebrews 12:16-17 says: " Lest there be any fornicator or profane person such as Esau, who for one morsel of meat sold his birthright."

It is true that at 77 years of age, Jacob was persuaded by his mother to deceive his father, but he did not steal the birthright. He did what he did to keep his brother, who had sold it to him, from stealing it. Compare Genesis 25:20-26 and Genesis 27:6-17.

It is interesting to note that the day Jacob had to flee for his life from Beersheba, he got as far as Bethel. Then God appeared to him in a dream (Genesis 28:13-15) and said, "I am the Lord God of Abraham thy father and the God of Isaac; the land whereon thou liest, to thee will I give it, and to thy seed… and in thee and "in thy seed" shall all the families of the earth be blest… For I will not leave thee until I have done that which I have spoken to thee of." The Bible only records one lie that Jacob told in 147 years (Genesis 27:19-24). How many of his critics can match that? Compare (Genesis 31:36-55).

Tradition # 7: The Greek word bema, translated as "judgment seat" in the King James version would be more correctly translated as "reward seat". That is why only rewards are given out at the podium (bema) at the Olympics.

(2 Corinthians 5:10) reads as follows: "For we must all appear before the judgment seat of Christ; that every one may receive the things done in his body, according to that he hath done, whether it be good or bad."

People who believe that a Christian cannot be punished, insist on calling the judgment seat of Christ "the *bema*" or the "reward seat of Christ". That way, a "bad act" can be softened up to mean a "worthless work". In other words, it is something that does not deserve a reward, but it does not need to be punished.

However, the word *bema* in *Strong's Concordance* means "a rostrum" or "a tribunal". Surely one would expect justice at a tribunal for the good or bad. That is the way it is used in the Bible.

In Acts 18:12-16, we read that Gallio drove the Jews from the judgment seat – the *bema.*

In Acts 18:17, it states: "Then all the Greeks took Sosthenes, the chief ruler of the synagogue, and beat him before the judgment seat – the *bema.*"

In John 19:13-16, we read that Pilate went into the judgment hall and sat down in the judgment seat – the *bema,* and after deliberating, he delivered Jesus to be crucified and scourged (Matthew 27:19–26).

This tradition clearly does not square with the Scriptures.

Tradition # 8: One thousand years is an indefinite period of time that cannot be determined because 2 Peter 3:8 says that "one day is with the Lord as a thousand years and a thousand years as one day."

This phrase is also found in Psalm 90:4: "For a thousand years in thy sight are but as yesterday when it is past and as a watch in the night." This sentiment is echoed in the words of Job 7:6 ("My days are swifter than a weaver's shuttle") and again in 9:25 ("My days are swifter than a post[1]").

We mortals, especially us old folks, can easily relate to these sayings. When we were children, we couldn't comprehend how long a year was. Now that we are old, it seems like yesterday when it is past.

If there is that much difference from childhood to adulthood, how much more between a mortal man and God? It is easy to imagine how 1,000 years to us mortals is only like a day to God.

How long is 1,000 years?

In round figures, it is 365,250 revolutions of the earth. In Genesis 1:14, it says: "And God said, 'Let there be lights in the firmament of the heaven to divide the day from the night; and let them be for signs, and for seasons, and for days, and years.'" Genesis 8:22 says:

---

1 "Post" as in Esther 3:15: "The posts went out being hastened by the king's commandment."

"While the earth remaineth, seedtime and harvest, and cold and heat, and summer and winter, and day and night, shall not cease."

Tradition # 9: Forty stripes will kill a man, hence when Paul was whipped they always stopped at 39 to be sure not to kill him.

This is folklore. Deuteronomy 25:3 says: "Forty stripes may he give him and not exceed: lest if he should exceed, and beat him above these with many stripes, then thy brother should seem vile unto thee."

Tradition #10: Peter asked to be crucified upside down because he was not worthy to be crucified in the same manner that his Lord was.

This too is folklore. Most churches know it and admit it, yet they cannot resist telling it. What benefit can come from teaching folklore in the pulpits of the churches?

I hope that the above examples have proved that some non-doctrinal traditions do not square with the Scriptures. In the following chapters, I hope to identify many more traditions that do not square with the scriptures.

CHAPTER TWO

The Sequence of Events Between the Rapture and the New Heaven and the New Earth

The primary message of this chapter, is to establish the **Time**, the **Place**, and the **Purpose** of the Judgment seat of Christ.

The chart on pages 18 and 19 shows the Place of the Judgment in relation to the other events.

The Time – is when Jesus returns to reign on this earth for 1,000 years immediately after the Tribulation period spoken of in Matthew 24: 29 and 30. The beast and the false prophet have been cast alive into the lake of fire (Revelation 19: 20) and Satan is held captive in the bottomless pit for 1,000 years (Revelation 20: 1 to 3).

The Place – will be on planet earth (Zechariah 14: 1 to 9). For out of Zion shall go forth the Law and the word of the Lord from Jerusalem (Isaiah 2: 3b).

The Purpose – is for every Christian to receive for the deeds done in the body since they were saved (Revelation 11: 15 and 18) whether those deeds were good or bad (Ecclesiastes 12: 14 and 2 Corinthians 5: 10 and 11a). Some will reign with Him (Romans 8: 17, 2 Timothy 2: 12 and Revelation 20: 4). Others will receive 100 fold (Matthew 19: 29). All rewards will be according to the work (Matthew 16: 27 and Revelation 22: 12).

Those who have done wrong will receive for the wrong they have done and there is no respect of persons (Colossians 3:25).

It is incomprehensive to me that this "Event" known as the "Judgement seat of Christ" An Event that will effect every Christian that has ever lived for 1000 years, is not even mentioned in any Statement of Faith that I have ever seen. Even those who believe in the Millennium, do not see it being the time when every Christian will receive for the deeds done in the body whether good or evil. (Ecclesiastes 12:14) (2 Corinthians 5:10–11)

Order of Events from

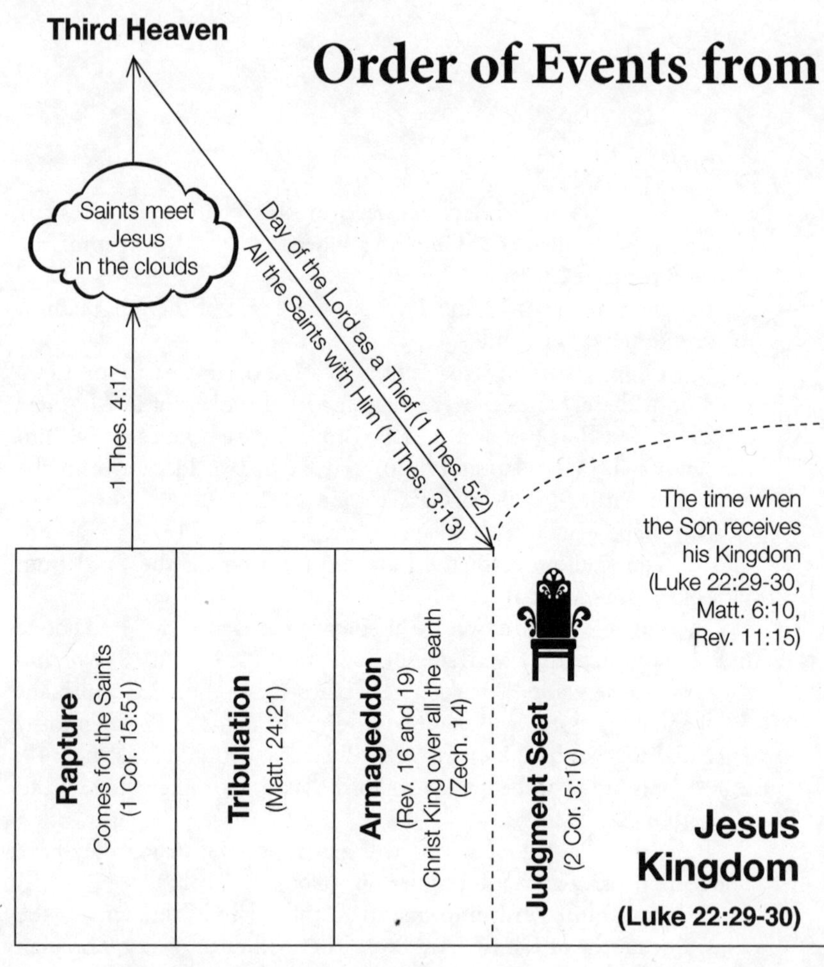

Rapture Pages 21-24
Main part of the first resurrection
Only saints are involved (Rev. 20:4-5)

Tribulation Page 24
The time of the antichrist

Armageddon Page 25
Beast and false prophet to Lake of Fire
Satan captive in Bottomless Pit

Judgment Seat Pages 26-30
Where saints learn about their rewards

Rapture to New Earth

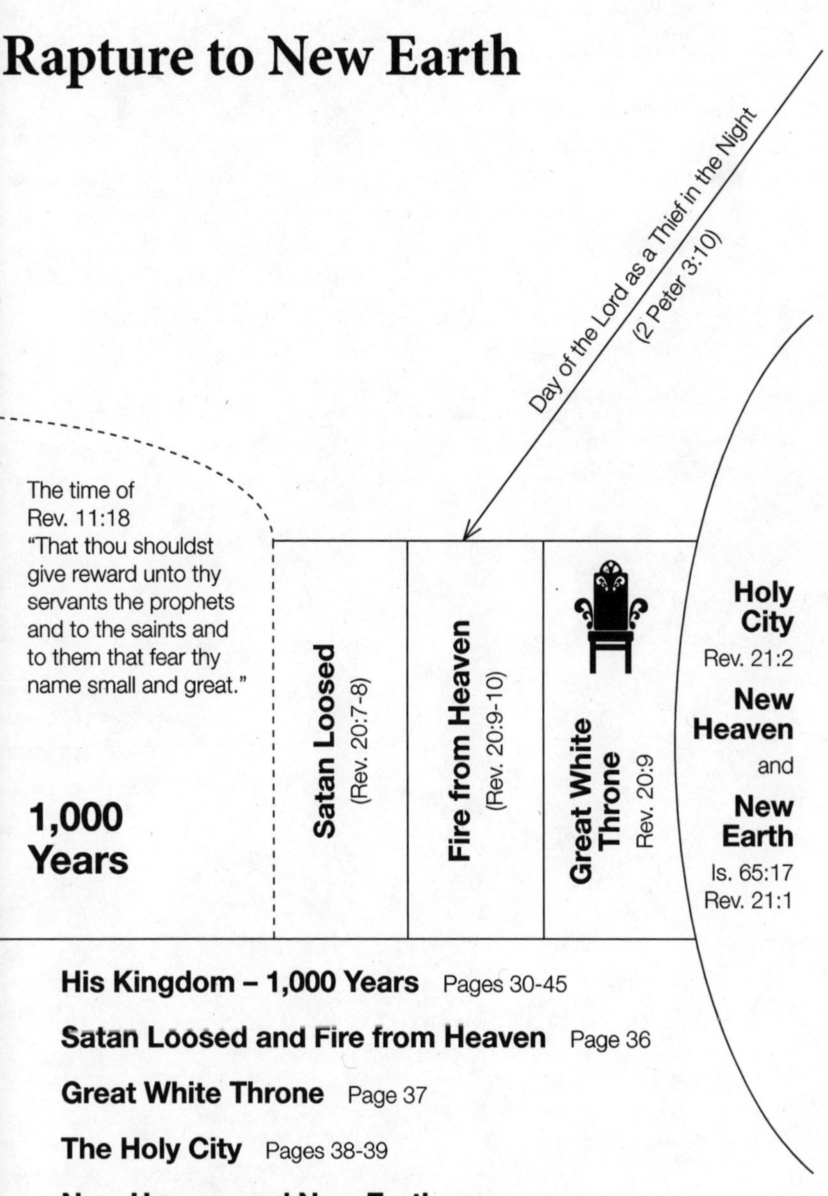

His Kingdom – 1,000 Years Pages 30-45

Satan Loosed and Fire from Heaven Page 36

Great White Throne Page 37

The Holy City Pages 38-39

New Heaven and New Earth Pages 39-40

Event #1: The Rapture

Many teach that references to the Lord's coming "for" the saints at the Rapture and His coming "with" the saints to reign, are so similar that one cannot be sure if they are two separate events, or if they occur at the same time. I find huge differences in the accounts of these two events.

- **At the Rapture**, He comes "for" the saints to take them to be with Him forever. (1 Corinthians 15:51 - 52 and 1 Thessalonians 4:17)

  When He comes to Reign, He brings all the saints "with" Him. (Zechariah 14:5 and 1 Thessalonians 3:13)

- **At the Rapture**, He does not actually come to earth. The saints are caught up to meet Him in the clouds. (1 Thessalonians 4:17)

  When He comes to Reign, He actually comes to earth and stands on the mount of Olives. (Zechariah 14: 4 - 5)

- **At the Rapture**, there is no mention of Him being seen by the people living on the earth.

  When He comes to Reign, every eye shall see Him. (Matthew 24: 30 and Revelation 1: 7)

- **At the Rapture**, there is no mention of a judgment of the just or the unjust.

  When He comes to Reign, there is a judgment of the living and of the dead (2 Timothy 4: 1). The living are the people who are living on the earth at that time (Matthew 25: 31 - 46). The dead, are the dead in Christ who were raptured and return with Him (1 Thessalonians 3: 13), to receive for the deeds done in the body whether good or bad (2 Corinthians 5:10 - 11a,

Matthew 16: 27, Matthew 19: 27 – 30, Matthew 24: 42 - 51, Matthew 25: 1 - 30, Revelation 22: 12). Those who died outside of Christ are not at this judgment because they are not resurrected until the 1,000 years have ended (Revelation 20 : 5).

- **At the Rapture**, before the tribulation, the "righteous" are "taken" to be with Lord (1 Thessalonians 4: 15) and are made immortal (1 Corinthians 15: 53). The "unrighteous" are left to dwell on the earth. There is no judgment at this time.

  When He comes to Reign, after the tribulation, (Matthew 24: 29 – 30) it is just the opposite. All the people are gathered, and sorted (Matthew 25: 32) The "unrighteous" are "taken" and cast into the lake of fire (Matthew 25: 41), and the "righteous" are left to inherit, and repopulate the earth, (Matthew 25: 33 – 34). Just as it was in the days when the flood came and took all the unrighteous away, and righteous Noah, was "left" to repopulate the earth, (Matthew 24: 37 – 39).

- **At the Rapture**, there no signs to indicate His coming, only the Shout, and the Voice of the archangel, and the Trump of God which may only take a few minutes (1 Thessalonians 4:16). Then it is over in the twinkling of an eye, at the last trump, (1 Corinthians 15: 51 - 54). So shall we ever be with the Lord.

  When He comes to Reign, there are signs in the sun and the moon and the stars (Luke 12: 25 - 26) and the great earthquake of (Isaiah 24: 12 and Revelation 16: 16 - 21). All the people on earth shall see Him coming in power and great glory, (Matthew 24: 29 - 30).

- **At the Rapture**, the man of sin has not been revealed (2 Thessalonians 2: 3 - 8) and the tribulation period does not begin until after the signing of the covenant of (Daniel 9:27). This leads us to believe that it is the Holy Spirit of God dwelling in all the saints that hinders the work of Satan. That influence is taken away when the saints are raptured. This will open the way for the beast to gain enough credibility to make the covenant of (Daniel 9:27).

- **When He comes to Reign**, the tribulation period is over (Matthew 24: 29) The beast and the false prophet have been cast into the Lake of fire (Revelation 19:20) Satan has been confined to the bottomless pit (Revelation 20:1 - 3) Christ returns in person to the Mount of Olives and becomes Lord over the whole earth (Zechariah 14: 1 - 9, Revelation 11: 15, 18)

QUESTIONS AND ANSWERS ABOUT THE RAPTURE

Are there any signs indicating when the Rapture will take place?

I do not know of any.

What did the disciples mean when they asked, "What shall be the sign of thy coming and the end of the world?"

There are two occasions that speak of His coming. One is when He comes **for** the saints (the **Rapture**) and the other is when He comes **with** the saints to **Reign** over the earth (His kingdom). When Jesus spoke of His coming, it was nearly always with reference to his coming **with** the saints to Reign.

The disciples were not thinking about the Rapture. It was always the kingdom that was on their minds. This is the kingdom He taught them to pray for as in Matthew 6:10 ("Thy kingdom come..."), Luke 22:29 ("I appoint unto you a kingdom..."), and Acts 1:6 ("...wilt thou at this time restore the kingdom to Israel?").

John 14:1-3 seems to be the only reference Jesus made about his coming **for** the saints. The details seem to have remained a mystery until Jesus revealed them to Paul after Paul was converted. (I Corinthians 15:51-52, I Thessalonians 4:13-17 and Galatians 1:11-16)

Is Matthew 24:29-41 a reference to the Rapture?

I believe the answer is no. In the days of Noah, the wicked were taken, and the righteous Noah and his family were left to repopulate the earth. In Matthew 24:39-41, it is the same: The wicked (goats) are taken to everlasting punishment and the righteous (sheep) are left to repopulate the earth.

At the Rapture, there is no judgment and no mention of the wicked. The dead in Christ shall rise first, and we who are alive and remain shall be caught up together with them in the air. (1 Thessalonians 4:16-17)

How can the rapture be a joyous occasion for us when millions of our fellow countrymen are being killed or wounded by collisions and crashes of cars and trucks and trains and planes and ships, etc.?

I do not believe that will happen. I believe that the rapture will be preceded by **a Shout** from heaven that will get the attention of every person on earth.

"Then the voice of the archangel" – I expect that whatever he says will motivate motor vehicles to pull over, control towers to put all planes waiting to land on hold and pilots to put their planes, trains and ships on auto pilot.

"Then the sound of the trumpet" (1 Thessalonians 4:13 to 16) – We do not know how long each of these events will last, but I believe it will be long enough for the whole world to come to a standstill. Then, in a moment in the twinkling of an eye, the saints will be gone (I Corinthians 15:52) and crashes and collisions and loss of life will be minimal.

I believe that millions of people that are left behind will hear and believe the testimony of the two witnesses (Revelation 11: 3 to 6) and be among the multitudes spoken of in Revelation 7: 9 to 17. We know that God is not willing that any should perish but that all should come to repentance (2 Peter 3:9b).

Event #2: The Tribulation Period

When all the believers are gone because of the Rapture, the hindering work of the Holy spirit that was in them is gone also. The beast is revealed with all power and signs and lying wonders (2 Thessalonians 2:7-9) and even able to call down fire from heaven (Revelation 13:13), so that people will say who is able to make war with him (Revelation 13:4).

Daniel 9:27 states that he makes a peace covenant with many for one week (seven years).

Revelation 11:3-13 says that two witnesses, who have miraculous power to defend themselves, prophesy (1 Corinthians 14:3) preaching the gospel for 42 months.

The beast makes an image that can speak (Revelation 11:3) and assigns a number to the image which people must have in order to buy or sell (Revelation 13:11-18). As a result of this law, multitudes are beheaded for their faith (Revelation 7:11-17). They cry out to God, asking when he will avenge their blood. (Revelation 6:9-11)

When the abomination of desolation spoken of by Daniel the prophet stands in the temple, the beast has run out of time (Revelation 10:6). The vengeance of God begins, and for the next forty-two months, there will be such great tribulation as was not since the beginning of the world. (Daniel 12:11 and Matthew 24:15-21)

Revelation 14:6-7 says, "And I saw another angel fly in the midst of heaven having the everlasting gospel to preach unto them that dwell on the earth, and to every nation and kindred and tongue and people."

The weapons the Lord uses to avenge the blood of the saints are not made by man. They are weapons over which humans have no defense: hail, fire, brimstone, pouring rain, burning sun, plagues, pestilences, creatures with tails like scorpions, pollution of rivers and seas by turning their waters to blood, darkening of the sun and the moon, earthquakes, and such a shaking of the heavens and earth that the stars fall from the heavens and mountains crumble. Even the earth reels on its axis like a drunkard, allies fight against one another, and others die of a flesh-eating disease. (Isaiah 24:20; Ezekiel 38:39; Zechariah 14; Revelation 6; 8 ; 9; 16)

In the final battle, the beast and the false prophet are cast alive into the lake of fire. (Revelation 19:20) Satan is captured and held captive in the bottomless pit for 1,000 years. (Revelation 20:1-3) And Christ is King over the whole earth (Zechariah 14:9) for 1000 years. (Revelation 20:4-6 and 1 Corinthians 15:25-28)

Event #3: Armageddon

According to Matthew 24:22, there is so much blood shed during the tribulation that except those days be shortened, there would be no life left. Those days are brought to a close by a final battle that seems to be fought on three fronts all over the land of Israel.

Armageddon is where the kings of the whole world will be gathered together to make war against the armies of heaven (Revelation 16:1-21 and Revelation 19:11-21) and Jerusalem (Zechariah 14:1–4) and the Mountains of Israel (Ezekiel 38:18-23 and Zechariah 14). The weapons the Lord uses are thunder, lightning, and an earthquake so mighty and so great such as was not seen since men were upon the earth. There will be hailstones weighing over 100 pounds. The whole earth will shake so that the mountains will crumble.

The earth will reel like a drunkard. (Isaiah 24:20) There will be pestilence, blood, an overflowing rain, fire and brimstone, and a plague that will cause "their flesh to consume away while they stand on their feet, their eyes to consume away in their holes, and their tongues to consume away in their mouths." Every man's sword will be against his brother. (Ezekiel 38:21 and Zechariah 14:13)

Half the city will be taken, and the houses rifled, and the women ravished. Then the Lord will come and all the saints with Him. When His feet stand on the Mount of Olives, it will be split down the middle with half moving to the north and half to the south, leaving a great valley in between. (Zechariah 14:1-4)

The beast and the false prophet will be taken and cast alive into the lake of fire, burning with brimstone. Satan will be captured and held captive in the bottomless pit for 1,000 years. (Revelation 19:20 and Revelation 20:2-3) In Matthew 24:29-30, we read that: "Immediately after the tribulation of those days, the sun will be darkened and the moon shall not give her light. The stars shall fall from heaven and the powers of the heaven shall be shaken. Then shall appear the sign of the Son of Man in heaven: and then shall all the tribes of the earth mourn, and they shall see the sign of the Son of Man coming in the clouds of heaven with power and great glory."

> *And the Lord shall be king over all the earth: in that day shall there be one Lord and his name one.* (Zechariah 14: 9)

> *Behold He cometh with clouds: and every eye shall see Him.* (Revelation 1:7)

Event #4: The Judgment Seat of Christ

This is the beginning of His kingdom (millennial kingdom). This is the kingdom of Luke 22:30 ("That ye may eat and drink at my table in my kingdom and sit on twelve thrones judging the twelve tribes of Israel.") and the kingdom he taught them to pray for in Matthew 6:10 ("Thy kingdom come. Thy will be done on earth as it is done in heaven.").

The judgment takes place on this earth, right after the tribulation when Christ is seated on the throne of his glory. (Matthew 19:28-30; Matthew 24:29-51; Matthew 25:1-46; 1 Corinthians 5:9-11a). It involves the "living" and the "dead" (the dead in Christ) who come with Him when He comes. (Zechariah 14; 5; 1; Thessalonians 3:13; 2 Timothy 4:1). The rest of the dead do not live again until the 1,000 years are finished. (Revelation 20:5)

An account of the judgment of the Living (2 Timothy 4: 1)

It includes all the people who are alive when Jesus comes and is seated on the throne of his glory. (Matthew 19:28 and Matthew 25:31) His angels gather all the nations and sorts them as a shepherd sorts the sheep from the goats. (Matthew 25:32-33) It will be like it was in the days of Noah when the flood came and took all the wicked away, and Noah and his family were left to replenish the earth. (Genesis 9:1; Matthew 24:37-41). At this judgment, the goats (the wicked) are cast into the lake of fire. (Matthew 25:41-46) The sheep (the righteous) are left to inherit the earth. They are still mortals and will repopulate the earth just as Noah did. (Matthew 25:33-34)

An account of the judgment of the Dead (2 Timothy 4: 1)

These are the dead in Christ who are raised at the first resurrection and come with him when He comes. (Zechariah 14:5; 1 Thessalonians 3:13; Revelation 20:6) This is when they will receive for the deeds done in the body according to what they have done whether good or bad. (2 Corinthians 5:10 -11a) The earth is regenerated, and Christ is seated on the throne of his glory. Matthew 19:27-28 and Luke 22:28-30 tell us about the 12 disciples who will have 12 thrones to judge the 12 tribes of Israel. Everyone who has forsaken houses or sisters or fathers or mothers for His sake will receive a hundred fold in this present world (during the millennium) and everlasting life in the world to come (the New Heaven and the New Earth) (Matthew 19:29 and Luke 18:28 -30)

Everyone will be fully recompensed for whatever good they do.

> *Whosoever shall give a drink to one of these little ones a cup of cold water only in the name of a disciple, verily I say unto you, he shall in no wise lose his reward.* (Matthew 10:42)

The words Heaven, Kingdom of Heaven, and Kingdom of God are most often used with reference to the 1,000-year reign of Christ over this earth. Jesus calls it His kingdom (2 Timothy 4: 1) He calls it the kingdom that is appointed to him (Luke 22: 29-30) The kingdom he taught them to pray for (Matthew 6: 10) The kingdom they were expecting him to restore to Israel (Acts 1: 6). This kingdom will come at the end of Armageddon (Revelation 11: 15) *That thou shouldest give reward unto thy servants the prophets and to the saints and to them that fear thy name both small and great* (Revelation 11: 18) *that they without us will not be made perfect* (Hebrews 11: 39 – 40).

Note that all saints are equal when they are presented to the Father in the new heaven and the new earth after the 1,000 years because the qualification for everyone is the same – "the righteousness of Christ" (Jude 24). All saints are not equal during the millennium because what they receive depends on the deeds they have done whether they be good or bad. (2 Corinthians 5:10–11, Matthew 19:30, Matthew 18:4)

Faithful servants receive rewards according to their faithfulness. (Matthew 24:42-47) Unfaithful servants receive punishment according to their unfaithfulness. (Matthew 24:48-51) Those servants who did their best with what they were given were rewarded according to their works. (Matthew 25:14-23) The servant who did not even try is called a "wicked and slothful servant" and is cast into outer darkness where there is weeping and gnashing of teeth. (Matthew 25:24-30)

God will avenge a brother who is defrauded by another brother. (1 Thessalonians 4:6)

Those who serve heartily as to the Lord and not to men "shall receive the reward of the inheritance for ye serve the Lord Christ". (Colossians 3:24)

> *But he that doeth wrong shall receive for the wrong that he hath done and there is no respect of persons.* (Colossians 3:25)

Saints who defile the temple of God will be destroyed (saved yet so as by fire). (1 Corinthians 3:15-17) Saints who do not repent of their sin are said to be carnal. They have defiled the temple of God. (1 Corinthians 6:18-20) They will not have any inheritance in his millennial kingdom. (1 Corinthians 6:9-10 and Ephesians 5:5)

I believe that what the Promised Land was to Israel is, in many ways, a picture of what the millennial kingdom is to us.

Many of the people did not get into the Promised Land because they fell (rebelled). Twenty-three thousand died a premature death because of their rebellion. Also the 603,548 men of war who rebelled at Kadesh died prematurely and did not get into the land. (Numbers 1:46; Numbers 14:28-30; and Numbers 26:64) Many more are listed in 1 Corinthians 10:1-12.

Even Moses and Aaron were denied entrance to the Promised Land because they rebelled (fell) and would not or could not repent. (Numbers 20–24, Deuteronomy 3:23-27, Hebrews 6:4-6, and Hebrews 12:16-17)

"Willful sin", "presumptuous sin", "rebellion", "despising His Word", "acts of defiance", and "falling away" are terms used for sins that God will not forgive. If the people of God do these, it is impossible to renew them to repentance. Like Moses and Aaron, they do not lose their status as children of God, but they have to bear their iniquity, so the account is settled. The punishment for willful sin must not be thought of as a natural consequence, as many teach. Miriam having leprosy for seven days was not a natural consequence for criticizing Moses, nor was dying prematurely a natural consequence of smiting the rock. It was fair and just punishment from God for the rebellion that was in their hearts. (Compare Hebrews 10:23-36 and Hebrews 6:4-6)

Whereas Moses was seen with Jesus on the mount of transfiguration, we know that not getting into the Promised Land (rest) did not affect his status as one of God's children. Likewise, if a saint fails to get into the millennial kingdom (rest) of (Hebrews 3: 18) (Hebrews 4: 1).

As those Israelites who fell (sinned willfully) did not get into the Promised Land, so we who fall (sin willfully) will not get into the millennial rest. (Hebrews 4:1, 5, 8, 9, 11) (Hebrews 10:23–30)

The fornicators (of 1 Corinthians 5:10) are regarded as non-Christians. They are not at this judgment because they are not resurrected until the 1,000 years are ended. (Revelation 20:5) The fornicators (of 1 Corinthians 5:11) are regarded as brothers, who have defiled the temple of God and therefore will be destroyed (punished) but "saved: yet so as by fire". (1 Corinthians 3:15 -17) They "will not have any inheritance in the kingdom of Christ and of God." (Ephesians 5:5)

Paul faithfully warned us about the danger of "falling" (1 Corinthians 10:1-12), of being a "castaway" (1 Corinthians 9:27), of "outer darkness" (Matthew 25:30), of "the terror of the Lord" (2 Corinthians 5:10-11a), and of the "vengeance of God on those who count the blood of the covenant wherewith they were sanctified an unholy thing" (Hebrews 10:23-31). All of these truths were taught by Jesus and Peter and John and Paul.

In spite of the above, there is a tradition that is widely taught throughout most of Christendom – that when the people of God die they are "absent from the body to be present with the Lord". This is true as per 2 Corinthians 5:8. From there, this tradition skips over the next six verses and bypasses the Judgment Seat of Christ. A reminder of this judgment is in (Hebrews 9:27). *It is appointed unto man once to die and after that the judgment.*

This tradition ignores the significance of the 1,000-year reign of Christ, which according to Revelation 11:15-18, is the time when all the saints of all the ages will receive for the deeds done in the body whether good or bad. This tradition takes all the saints just as they are, regardless of how they have lived (any bad work they may have done was covered at the cross, and they have nothing to fear), to the New Heaven and the New Earth, where "God shall wipe away all tears from their eyes; and there shall be no more death, neither sorrow or crying, neither shall there be any more pain: for the former things are passed away.

Is it any wonder that the carnal Christian sees no reason to give up the pleasures of sin? He has been taught that he has nothing to fear.

How do the proponents of this tradition explain Ezekiel 3:20, which says: "When a righteous man doth turn from his righteousness, and commit iniquity, and I lay a stumbling block before him, he shall die: because thou hast not given him warning, he shall die in his sin, and his righteousness which he hath done shall not be remembered; but his blood will I require at thine hand."

Event #5: Jesus Kingdom

When does it start? It begins as soon as Armageddon is over and Satan is held captive in the bottomless pit and *the kingdoms of this world are become the kingdoms of our Lord and of his Christ* (Revelation 11: 15) *and the Lord shall be king over all the earth* (Zechariah 14: 9) Jesus called it *the regeneration when the Son of man will sit on the throne of his glory* (Matthew 19: 28) He called it His kingdom *And I appoint unto you a kingdom as my father has appointed me; that you may eat and drink with me at my table in my kingdom, and sit on thrones judging the twelve tribes of Israel* (Luke 22: 29 – 30) He taught them to pray for it; *Thy kingdom come, thy will be done on earth as it is done in heaven* (Matthew 6: 10).

How long will it last? One **thousand** years. *And he laid hold on the dragon that old serpent called the devil and Satan and bound him a* ***thousand*** *years, that he should deceive the nations no more till the* ***thousand*** *years should be fulfilled. And the souls that were beheaded lived and reigned with Christ a* ***thousand*** *years. All who are in the first resurrection shall reign with him a* ***thousand*** *years. But the rest of the dead lived not again until the* ***thousand*** *years were finished. And when the* ***thousand*** *years are expired Satan shall be loosed out of his prison* (Revelation 20: 2 – 7) compare page 12.

When does it end? *He must reign until he has put all enemies under his feet and the last enemy to be destroyed is death* (1 Corinthians 15: 25 – 26) (Revelation 20: 10) *then shall the Son also be subject unto him that put all things under him that God may be all in all* (1 Corinthians 15: 28) *But the day of the Lord will so come as a thief in the night in which the heavens will pass away with a great noise and the elements shall melt with fervent heat and the earth also and the works that are therein shall be burned up* (2 Peter 3: 10).

How will this affect the saints? During this thousand year kingdom, every Christian that ever lived will be resurrected and fully recompensed for the deeds done in the body, whether good or bad. Some will receive a hundred fold for what they have done for Him (Matthew 19: 29)

As for the bad - *For God will bring every work into judgment whether it be good or whether it be evil* (Ecclesiastes 12: 14) *For we must all appear before the judgment seat of Christ; that every one may receive the things done in his body according to that he hath done whether it be good or bad,* (2 Corinthians 5: 10) *He that doeth wrong shall receive for the wrong that he hath done and there is no respect of persons* (Colossians 3: 25) *And the time of the dead that they should be judged, and that thou shouldst give reward unto thy servants the prophets and the saints and them that fear thy name both small and great* (Revelation 11: 18).

It is appointed unto men once to die, and after that the judgment (Hebrews 9: 27)

Some men's sins are judged in this life such as Miriam and Annanias and some who who ate and drank unworthily, but not all accounts are settled in this life. *Some men's sins are open beforehand going before to judgment and some they follow after* (1 Timothy 5: 24)

How can an event that will affect every Christian that ever lived for a thousand years get so little attention from the leaders of the flocks? Have they not read (Ezekiel 3: 20) ?

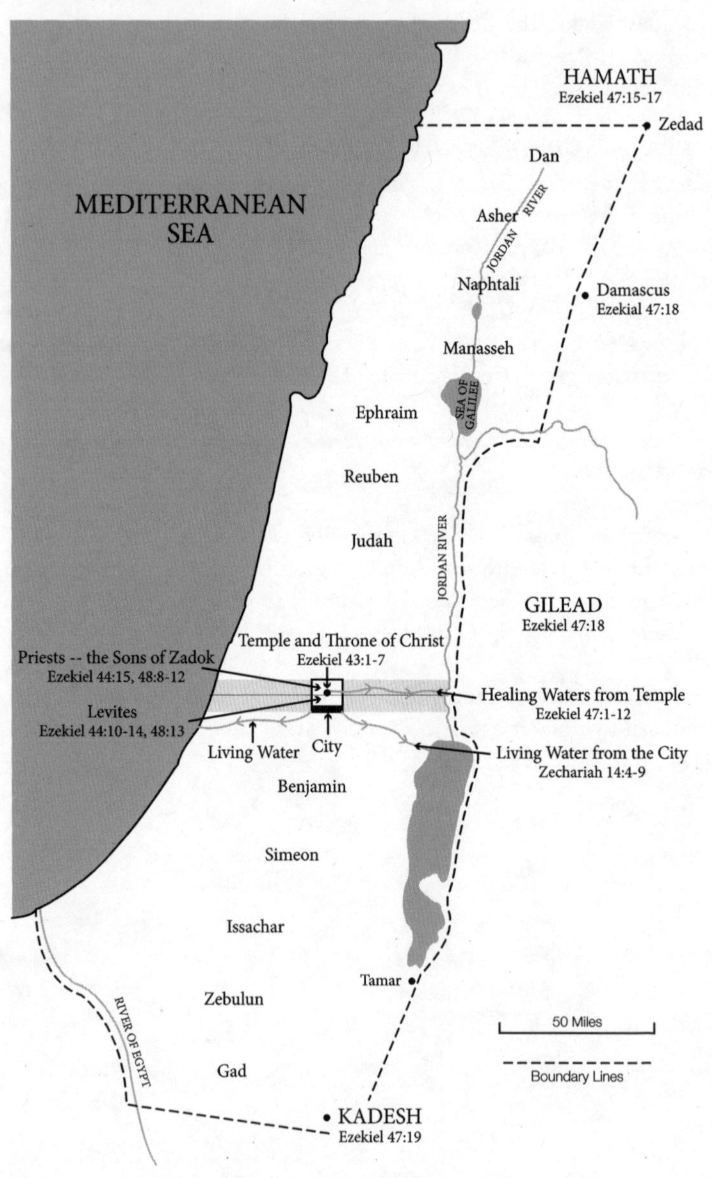

Location of the twelve tribes during Millennium

About the Millennium

Jesus called it "the Regeneration". (Matthew 19:28) Peter called it "the times of refreshing that shall come from the presence of the Lord" (Acts 3:19) and "the times of the restitution of all things which God hath spoken of all his holy prophets since the world began" (Acts 3:21).

The earth will be delivered from the curse of Genesis 3:17-39. There will be no more thorns and thistles, the wilderness will be like Eden, and the desert will be like the garden of God. (Isaiah 51:3) People will say, "This land that was desolate is like the garden of Eden." (Ezekiel 36:35) The land will be called Beulah. There will be rivers in high places, fountains in the valleys, and trees in the desert. There will be streams in the desert, the lame will leap, and the dumb will speak. (Isaiah 35:1-7) Instead of the thorn and the briar, there will be the fir tree and the myrtle tree. The mountains and the hills will break forth into singing and the trees will clap their hands. (Isaiah 55:12-13)

> *The creature also will be delivered from the bondage of corruption into the glorious liberty of the children of God.* (Romans 8:19-21)

> *The wolf also shall dwell with the Lamb, and the leopard shall lie down with the Kid; and the calf and the young lion and the fatling together; and a little child shall lead them. And the cow and the bear shall feed; their young ones shall lie down together: and the Lion shall eat straw like the ox. And the suckling child shall play on the hole of the asp, and the weaned child shall put his hand on the cockatrice den.* (Isaiah 11:6-9)

Only the serpent is not delivered, as "dust shall be the serpent's meat." (Isaiah 65:25)

The people will live longer "for as the days of a tree are the days of my people." (Isaiah 65:22)

The nations will be at peace. As in Isaiah 2:4: "They will beat their swords into plowshares and their spears into pruning hooks: neither shall they learn war any more." The Israelites will be named "the priests of the Lord" (Isaiah 61:5 -6) and "the Gentiles shall serve them" (Isaiah 60:1-14).

It will be a just and righteous kingdom.

> *And He shall not judge after the sight of His eyes, neither reprove after the hearing of his ears: but with righteousness shall He judge the poor, and reprove with equity for the*

> *meek of the earth: and he shall smite the earth with the rod of His mouth and with the breath of his lips shall He slay the wicked. And righteousness shall be the girdle of His loins and faithfulness the girdle of His reins.* (Isaiah 11:1-5) (See also Zechariah 14:16-19 and Revelation 2:27.)

QUESTIONS AND ANSWERS ABOUT JESUS KINGDOM

Can a Christian ever lose his salvation?

The answer is "no". No one who has been born of the Spirit can lose his salvation because of God's guarantee:

In whom also after that ye believed ye were sealed with that Holy Spirit of promise, which is the earnest (guarantee) of our inheritance until the redemption of the purchased possession, unto the praise of His glory. (Ephesians 1:13b-14) This guarantee is repeated three times – in Ephesians 4:30, 2 Corinthians 1:22, and 2 Corinthians 5:5.

Doesn't 1 Corinthians 6:9 say that, "The unrighteous shall not inherit the kingdom of God," and 1 Corinthians 6:10 say that, "Thieves, nor covetous, nor drunkards, nor revilers, nor extortioners, shall inherit the kingdom of God," and Ephesians 5:5 say that, "No whoremonger, nor unclean person, nor covetous man who is an idolater, hath any inheritance in the kingdom of Christ and of God"?

The answer is: Yes, they do. However, the literal aspect of the kingdom of God spoken of here, and in most places, is with reference to the millennial kingdom, where all the people of God will receive for the deeds done in the body whether good or bad. That is the context of the above quotations. Just as thousands of the people of God that came out of Egypt (including Miriam, Moses, and Aaron) did not get into the Promised Land, thousands of the people of God who are living after the flesh and not after the Spirit will not get into the millennial kingdom. And just as Moses did not lose his status as one of God's people, so these carnal Christians will not lose their status as people whose bodies are the temple of God.

> *What! know ye not, that your body is the temple of the Holy Ghost which is in you, which ye have of God and ye are not your own? For ye are bought with a price: therefore glorify*

God in your body and in your spirit which are God's. (1 Corinthians 6:19-20)

These people will not get into His kingdom. They will receive for the wrong that they have done (Colossians 3:25), and when the thousand years are over, they will be transferred to the New Heaven and the New Earth where all their tears will be wiped away (Revelation 21:4).

Apart from the millennium, there is no place in the Bible timeline for any meaningful judgment.

The question we must answer is: Why are we not warning the righteous who have turned from their righteousness as Ezekiel was told to do (Ezekiel 3:20) and as Jesus, Peter, John, and Paul did throughout the New Testament?

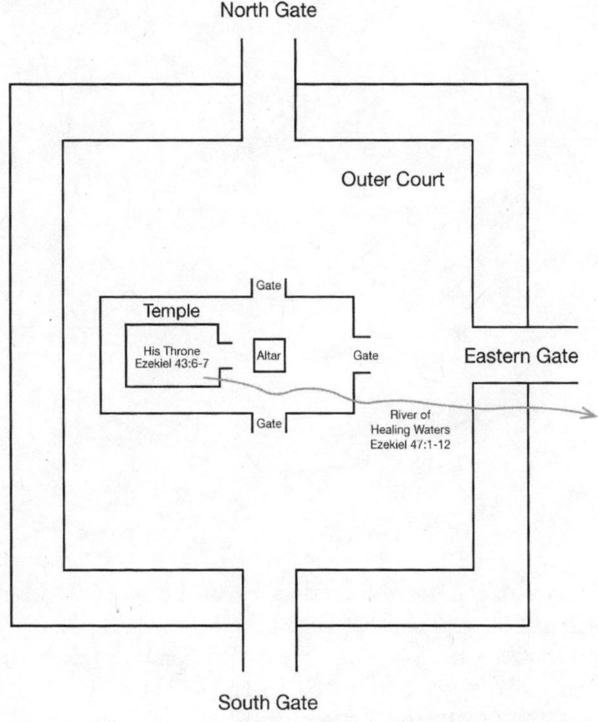

Temple of the 1,000-Year Kingdom (Ezekiel 42:15-20; 44:1-4)
The Temple area is one square mile

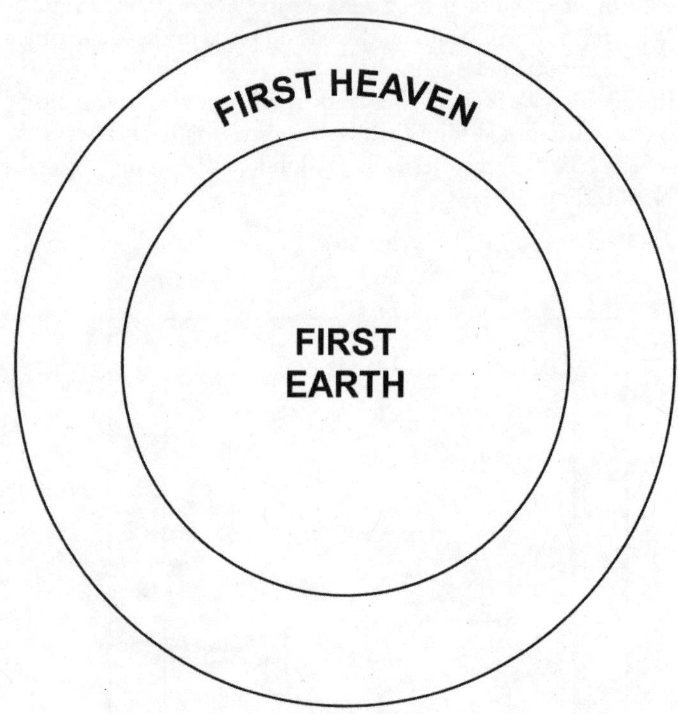

What we receive for the deeds done in the body will be received during the 1,000-year reign of Christ on this earth. (Luke 22:28-30)

Shortly after the 1,000 years are ended, some people born during that period will decide to follow Satan, and will be destroyed in the fire of Revelation 20:7-10 and 2 Peter 3:7-10.

Those remaining will be the kingdom that the Son turns over to the Father. (1 Corinthians 15:25-28)

I think they will be in the Holy City when it descends to the New Earth. (Revelation 21:10)

Event #6: Satan Loosed and Fire from Heaven

Peter prophesied that the heavens and earth are reserved unto fire against the Day of Judgment and perdition of ungodly men. That prophecy is fulfilled at the end of the 1,000 years of His reign on this earth. (2 Peter 3:7 and Revelation 20:7-10)

1 Corinthians 15:25 and 15:26 says that Christ must reign until all enemies are put under His feet. The last enemy to be destroyed is death (Satan).

> *And when the thousand years are expired, Satan shall be loosed out of his prison and shall go out to deceive the nations which are in the four quarters of the earth, Gog and Magog, to gather them together to battle: the number of whom is as the sand of the sea. And they went up on the breadth of the earth, and compassed the camp of the saints about, and the beloved city: and the fire came down from God out of Heaven, and devoured them.* (Revelation 20:7-9)

> *But the day of the Lord will come as a thief in the night; in which the heavens shall pass away with a great noise, and the elements shall melt with fervent heat, the earth also and the works that are therein shall be burned up.* (2 Peter 3:10)

The devil who deceived them is cast into the lake of fire and brimstone where the beast and false prophet are (and have been for 1,000 years) and shall be tormented day and night forever and ever (Revelation 19:20, 20:10).

According to Isaiah (Isaiah 65:20–22), during His 1,000-year reign, long life is restored.

The "sheep" who survive the tribulation will inherit the earth as mortals and will repopulate the earth just as Noah did after the flood. (Matthew 24: 37–38 and Matthew 25:31-34)

Those mortals that do not follow Satan, will, along with all of the redeemed of the ages be the kingdom that Christ delivers to God in the Holy city that descends to the new earth as a bride adorned for her husband (Revelation 20:1-4). Note that there are over three billion cubic miles of space in this city.

Event #7: The Great White Throne

I believe no one deserves to be tormented day and night forever and ever because of any bad deed that is done in the body. I am confident that the Lord can and will be able to fully recompense any such deed within the 1,000 years of His reign.

If anyone is sent to the lake of fire, it will be because they knowingly and willfully rejected what God has revealed to them about Himself so that they are without excuse. (Romans 1:17-20)

> *He that believeth not the Son shall not see life but the wrath of God abideth on him.* (John 3:36)

Revelation 13:8 says that if one rejects the Lamb of God, slain from the foundation of the world, he is certain to incur the wrath of God. (John 3:18, 3:36, 12:48)

After the 1,000 years are expired, Satan will be loosed and will gather a mighty army to come against the Holy City. Fire coming down from God out of Heaven will destroy them. The devil who deceived them will be cast into the lake of fire where the beast and false prophet have been for 1,000 years. (2 Peter 3:10, Revelation 19:20, Revelation 20:7-10).

> *And I saw a great white throne, and him that sat on it, from whose face the earth and the heaven fled away; and there was found no place for them. And I saw the dead, small and great, stand before God; and the books were opened: and another book was opened, which is the book of life: and the dead were judged out of those things which were written in the books, according to their works. And the sea gave up the dead which were in it; and death and hell gave up the dead which were in them: and they were judged every man according to their works. And death and hell were cast into the lake of fire. This is the second death. And whosoever was not found written in the book of life was cast into the lake of fire. (*Revelation 20:11-15)

To reject the blood of the Lamb of God (Hebrews 9:22) who endured the cross, despising the shame (Hebrews 12:2) so that any repentant sinner could have his sins forgiven (Luke 24:46-47), is sure to evoke the wrath of God (John 3:36).

Event #8: The Holy City

The Holy City, the new Jerusalem, comes down from God out of Heaven (Revelation 21:2) and settles on the New Earth. (Ezekiel 43:7; Revelation 21:10)

Moses' tabernacle for God was a cube (10 x 10 x 10 cubits).

Solomon's tabernacle for God was a cube (20 x 20 x 20 cubits).

Millennial tabernacle for His throne will be a cube (20 x 20 x 20 cubits).

The Holy City (His tabernacle) will be a cube (Revelation 21:3 and Revelation 16-17): 1,500 x 1,500 x 1,500 miles.

There is no temple and no veil to curtain Him off from His people. (Revelation 21:22) As the glory of God filled the tabernacle of Moses with light (Exodus 40:34-35), and the glory of God filled the tabernacle of Solomon with light (1 Kings 8:10-11), and the glory of the Lord filled the millennial temple with light (Ezekiel 43:1-7), so the glory of God will fill the Holy City with light – all 3,375,000,000 (three billion, three hundred and seventy-five million) cubic miles of it (Revelation 21:23).

The base of the city equals 2,250,000 square miles. This would cover two-thirds of the United States of America. (Revelation 21:16) Whereas the saints with bodies like unto His glorious body that are not bound by gravity, 30 billion of them could be within the walls of that City, and there would be less than 10 for every cubic mile. (Philippians 3:21)

No wonder God has promised to create a New Heaven and a New Earth. (Isaiah 65:17) Surely the present heaven and earth today would be totally inadequate for a city of such magnitude.

The saints are not restricted to spending eternity within the walls of the city. There are twelve gates that are never shut. (Revelation 21:12 and Revelation 21:25) Kings of the earth and nations will bring their glory and honor into it. (Revelation 21:24-27). The street of the city is pure gold as if it were transparent glass. (Revelation 21:21) There is no temple. The Lord God Almighty and the Lamb are the temple. (Revelation 21:22) A pure river of the water of life, clear as crystal, proceeds out from the throne of God and of the Lamb (Revelation 22:1-2) and down the midst of the street. On either side of the river is the tree of life, which bares twelve manners of fruit. It yields fruit every month, and the leaves of the tree are for the healing of the nations.

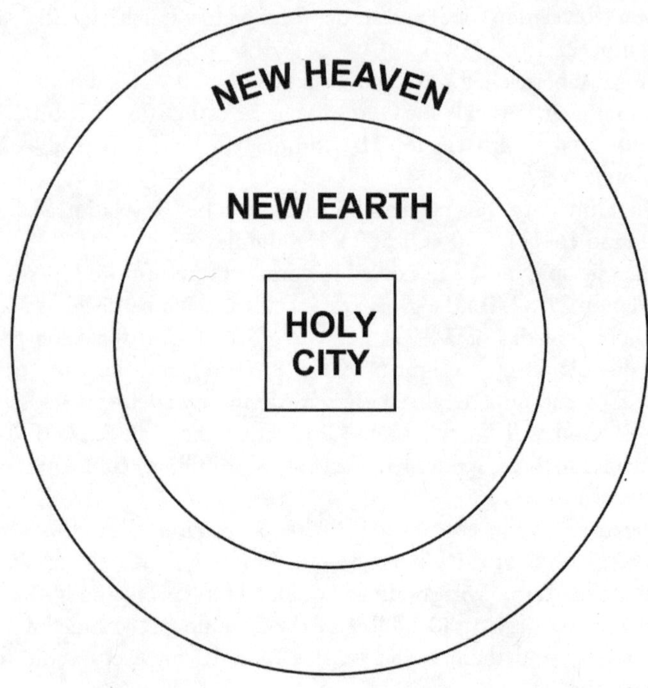

There is no night there, and the whole city of 3,375,000,000 cubic miles is lit by the glory of God. (Revelation 21:3, 5, 23) Just as the tabernacle in the wilderness and Solomon's tabernacle were lit, the tabernacle of the millennium will be lit by the glory of God.

Event #9: New Heaven and the New Earth

> *And I saw a new heaven and a new earth: for the first heaven and the first earth were passed away; and there was no more sea.* (Revelation 21:1)

I believe that the heat required to completely burn the mountains will vaporize the oceans, so that there will be no more sea where the first heaven and the first earth were. (See 1 Kings 18:38).

> *... The heavens shall pass away with a great noise, and the elements shall melt with fervent heat, the earth also and the works that are therein shall be burned up.* (2 Peter 3:10)

In Matthew 24:35, Jesus said, "Heaven and earth shall pass away, but my word shall not pass away."

> *For behold, I create new heavens and new earth: and the former shall not be remembered, nor come into mind.* (Isaiah 65:17)

> *For as the new heavens and the new earth, which I will make, shall remain before me, saith the Lord, so shall your seed and your name remain.* (Isaiah 66:22)

At the beginning of the 1,000 years, God will send His angels to gather all nations together, and He will sort the just from the unjust as a shepherd sorts the sheep from the goats. (Matthew 24:31, 25:31-32)

At the end of the 1,000 years when Satan is loosed, the ***unjust*** (unrighteous) who were born to the "sheep" during the 1,000 years will sort themselves by following Satan, who will gather them together to attack the beloved city. Fire from God will destroy them, along with the whole earth. (2 Peter 3:10 and Revelation 20:7-10)

The ***just*** (righteous) come to a New Earth in the Holy City – the new Jerusalem that John saw coming down from God out of heaven as a bride adorned for her husband. (Revelation 21:2) The City settles on the New Earth that God will create. (Isaiah 65:17 and Revelation 21:3)

Christ must reign until all enemies are put under His feet, then shall the Son also be subject unto Him who put all things under Him that God may be all in all. (1 Corinthians 15:25, 28) This is the time when the Son presents us (in His righteousness) faultless before the presence of His glory with exceeding joy. (Jude 24)

Event #10: When the Tears Are Wiped Away

There are just over one thousand years between the second coming (Zechariah 14:9), when He stands on the Mount of Olives and becomes King over all the earth, and the day of the fire (Revelation 20:9) that comes down from heaven so that "the heavens pass away with a great noise and the earth and the works that are in it are burned up." (2 Peter 3:10) Then the New Heaven and the New Earth are created. (Isaiah 65:17 and Revelation 21:1)

And God shall wipe away all tears from their eyes; and there shall be no more death, neither sorrow, nor crying, neither shall there be any more pain: for the former things are passed away. (Revelation 21:4)

Does this mean the tears are wiped away as soon as we go to be with the Lord (2 Corinthians 5:6)?

No, only our souls go to be with the Lord when we die. I believe the tears are the result of Christians (who knew the Lord's will and did not do it) receiving for the bad at the judgment seat of Christ. (Matthew 24:44-51)

The saints will get new immortal bodies when Jesus comes **for** them. (1 Corinthians 15:51-53 and Philippians 3:21) They come **with** Him when He comes to reign for 1,000 years. (Zechariah 14:5 and 1 Thessalonians 3:13)

And, behold I come quickly; and my reward is with me, to give to every man according as his work shall be. (Revelation 22:12) (Revelation 11:15–18)

It is during the millennium that all the saints will have been fully recompensed for the deeds done in the body, whether they be good or bad. (2 Corinthians 5:10-11a)

The servant who knew the Lord's will and did not do it is beaten with many stripes. There will be weeping and gnashing of teeth. (Matthew 24:48-51 and Luke 12:47) The foolish virgins who let their lights go out by living after the flesh cut themselves off from fellowship with God and are told that He does not know them. Yet they will be saved, so as by fire. (Matthew 25:1-12 and 1 Corinthians 3:15) The unprofitable servant who buried his talent is cast into outer darkness where there is weeping and gnashing of teeth. (Matthew 25:30) The vengeance of God will come upon a brother who defrauds another brother. (1 Thessalonians 4:6) Those who trample the Son of God underfoot and count the blood of the covenant wherewith they were sanctified an unholy thing will experience the fearful vengeance of God. (Hebrews 10:29-31)

When the 1,000 years are over and every saint has been recompensed for the deeds done in the body, whether good or bad, and this heaven and earth have been burned up, and Satan has been cast into the lake of fire, the New Heaven and Earth are created. It is then that the Son turns the kingdom over to God, the Father (1 Corinthians 15:28), and the tears will be wiped away. There will be no more sorrow, crying, or death, for the former things are passed away (Revelation 21:4).

CHAPTER THREE
Other Traditions that do not Square with the Scriptures

This chapter reviews more traditions that do not square with the Scriptures because some influential person (or persons) was negligent in searching the Scriptures to see if these things are so.

Traditions related to Abraham and Lot

> *And Terah lived seventy years, and begat Abram, Nahor, and Haran.* (Genesis 11:26)

How do we know that Haran was older than Nahor and would have been born when Terah was seventy?

Genesis 11:29 to 31 says that Haran begat Milcah, Isca, and Lot. Nahor married Haran's daughter Milcah, so we can assume that Haran was older than Nahor.

Genesis 11:32 says that Terah was 205 years old when he died. Genesis 12:4 tells us that when Terah died at age 205, Abram was 75 years old. So we conclude that Terah was 130 when Abram was born, and that Haran would have been 60 years older than Abram.

If we read Genesis 11:10 to 25, we learn that all of Haran's ancestors had their first son on or before they were 35 years old. If Lot was born when Haran was 35, Lot would be **25** years older than Abram and could easily have been 30 years older.

How can one justify ignoring the list of Abram, Nahor, and Haran in Genesis 11:26?

The Bible does not always list children in the order they were born. In Genesis 5:32 and 10:1, the sons of Noah are said to be Shem, Ham, and Japheth. However, from Genesis 10:21, we learn that Japheth is the eldest, born when Noah was 500 years old. Shem, who became 100 years old two years after the flood, was born when Noah was 502 (Genesis 11:10). Ham is called the younger son (Genesis 9:22-24).

Therefore, the order of birth of Noah's sons is Japheth, Shem, and Ham. Likewise, the order of birth of Terah's sons is Haran, Nahor, and Abram.

Tradition that Lot was selfish

> *And delivered just Lot, vexed with the filthy conversation of the wicked: For that righteous man dwelling among them, in seeing and hearing, vexed his righteous soul from day to day with their unlawful deeds.* (2 Peter 2:7-8)

I believe that Lot knew that the whole land of Canaan had been promised to Abraham's seed. He also knew that the best land in Canaan at that time was from Hebron to Beersheba where Abram finally settled after they were separated. As I see it, they both agreed that they had to separate, and Abram, out of respect for Lot's age (he was at least 20 years older than Abram) and integrity, offered Lot his choice of any place in the land of Canaan.

I believe that Lot knew that the day would come when all the land of Canaan would be filled with Abram's seed and, though he could have chosen Hebron or Beersheba, it seems that he never even considered that an option. He looked for land that had grass and a place where his "seed" would never need to be in conflict with Abram's "seed".

Why did he move into the city?

I think that in those times, the people had to live in cities, preferably walled ones, for protection. This was the practice all over Europe for generations. Living in an idolatrous city did not make Lot a Sodomite any more than living in Hebron made Abram a Canaanite. I believe that the king of Sodom recognized his integrity just as God did and made Lot a judge. That is why he was sitting in the gate (where judges sat) when the two angels came. Also, because he was a righteous man, he pressed upon them greatly to spend the night at his house. (Genesis 19:1-3)

Abram passed the extreme test of Mt 10: 37; God spared his son
Lot passed the same extreme test, and God spared his daughters
God spared Zoar because Lot found grace in His sight – Ge 19: 19;
Yet many revere righteous Abram, & despise righteous Lot, Why
Compare – (1 Samuel 2: 12 – 17, 22 – 34) (4: 10 -18)

Traditions related to Abram's seed in Egypt

Why do you say that the Israelites did not dwell in Egypt for 430 years? (Exodus 12:41)

God promised Abram that his "seed" would be strangers in a land not their own for 400 years. They would be afflicted and would come out of the land of affliction in the fourth generation. (Genesis 15:13-16)

The four generations recorded in Exodus 6:16-20 are Levi, Kohath, Amram, and Moses.

Whereas Kohath was one of the 70 who came to Egypt, we will assume that he was a newborn.

Amram, his son, had to be born by the time Kohath died at age 133. (Exodus 6:16)

Moses had to be born by the time Amram died at age 137. (Exodus 6:20)

We know that they came out of Egypt when Moses was age 80. (Exodus 7:7)

Thus, the maximum number of years they could have been in Egypt was 350.

This proves that the 400 years could not have started the day they went to Egypt. There has to be another starting date for the 400 years. From Genesis 15:13, we understand that Abram's 'seed' was to be strangers in a land not their own for 400 years.

Genesis 21:12 says: "… in Isaac shall thy 'seed' be called." Therefore, the 400 years would have started with the birth of Isaac. Isaac was born in the land of Canaan and never once left the land of Canaan, not even to get a wife. (Genesis 24:4-8). He died in the land of Canaan after 180 years. (Genesis 35:27-29) Whereas Jacob was born when Isaac was 60 (Genesis 25:26), Jacob would have been 120 years old when his father died. Jacob was 130 when he went to Egypt ten years later. (Genesis 47:8-9) The total time that Abram's seed were strangers sojourning in the land of Canaan was 180 + 10 = 190 years. That would leave 210 years for them to sojourn in the land of Egypt.

However, the whole history of the children of Israel who dwelt in Egypt started with the call of Abram in Ur of the Chaldees, exactly 430 years before the day they left Egypt (Exodus 12:41). This is confirmed in Acts 7:2-4, Genesis 12:1-3, and Galatians 3:17.

From where do we get the extra 30 years? When Abram left Haran, he was 75 years old. (Genesis 12:4) Isaac was born 25 years later. (Genesis 21:5) From the time of the call of Abram until he left Haran would have been five years.

5 + 25 + 190 + 210 = 430

I believe the translators got all the words correct, but if they had read the whole story ahead of time, they would have assembled those words to better reflect the way it was.

The Concept of Law and Grace

Is it true that the grace of God was not available to repentant sinners until Jesus came?

I do not think so. I do not believe there is anything in the Bible to support the tradition that in Old Testament times there was a "Dispensation of Law without Grace", or that we are now in a "Dispensation of Grace without Law".

As I see it, throughout the Bible, law and grace have worked side by side to draw us to God and save us from our sins. The law serves to convince us that we are sinners. Repentant sinners have always found grace in the eyes of the Lord.

The coats of skin God made for Adam and Eve were evidence of the grace of God. Noah found grace in the eyes of the Lord. Jonah testified to the grace of God in saving the people of Nineveh when they repented. The Israelites were beneficiaries of the grace of God many times in accordance with the covenant He made with them at Sinai as summarized in Leviticus 26.

When Adam ate of the forbidden fruit, he immediately knew he had done wrong and tried to hide. From that point, all of his descendants inherited an inborn sense of "right and wrong". This is evident in the following:

> *For when the Gentiles, which have not the law, do by nature the things contained in the law, these, having not the law, are a law unto themselves: which show the work of the law written in their hearts, their conscience also bearing witness, and their thoughts the mean while accusing or else excusing one another.* (Romans 2:14-15)

Likewise, the grace of God is evident in the following:

> *Come now, and let us reason together, saith the Lord: though your sins be as scarlet, they shall be as white as snow; though they be red like crimson, they shall be as wool.* (Isaiah 1:18)

Let the wicked forsake his way, and the unrighteous man his thoughts: and let him return unto the Lord, and he will have mercy upon him; and to our God, for he will abundantly pardon. (Isaiah 55:7)

We have the same manifestation of law and grace in the New Testament. On the day of His resurrection, Jesus said to his disciples:

And that repentance and remission of sins should be preached in His name among all nations, beginning at Jerusalem. (Luke 24:47)

In conclusion, the law written in our hearts (our conscience) convicts us of our sin. If we have quenched or turned a deaf ear to our conscience, we still have the moral laws written in the New Testament.

If we respond to the conviction of the law and confess our sins, He (by His grace) is faithful and just to forgive us our sins and to cleanse us from all unrighteousness.
(1 John 1:9)

For by grace are ye saved through faith; and that not of yourselves: it is the gift of God: not of works, lest any man should boast. (Ephesians 2:8-9)

The Law brings conviction to the soul. Grace makes repentant sinners whole. Law and grace, Law and grace, They go together like Lavender and Lace.

The New Man

Whosoever is born of God doth not commit sin; for his seed remaineth in him: and he cannot sin, because he is born of God. (1 John 3:9 – King James Version)

In 1 John 3:9, does the "interpolation" of the words "practice" or "continue", as found in some translations of this verse, square with the context or with the manuscript used by the authors of the King James Version of the Bible?

I do not see how they can. It appears that neither Strong nor his associates ever found any of the words in question in the manuscript that they used. This interpolation fails to resolve the problem because most Christians practice sin in one form or another. There are busybodies, gossips, gluttons, talebearers, procrastinators, faultfinders, and those who are covetous, envious, dishonest, and self-centered. And many Christians, to this day, habitually practice the violation of speed limits.

We have a whole list of sins in 1 Corinthians 5:11-13 and 6:1-20 that people in the church in Corinth were practicing, yet they are reminded that their bodies are the temple of God. I believe that the new man who is born of the Spirit (born again) is a spiritual man who did not exist before. (John 3:5-6) He is a spiritual man who is created after God in righteousness and true holiness. (Ephesians 5:24) 1 Peter 1:23 speaks of those who are "born again, not of corruptible seed, but of incorruptible, by the word of God, which liveth and abideth forever."

1 John 3:6 says: "Whosoever abideth in Him sinneth not." This spiritual man who is born of God does not sin because His seed (the Holy Spirit, Ephesians 1:13) remains in him, and he cannot sin because he is born of God. (1 John 3:9)

1 John 5:18 says: "Whosoever is born of God sinneth not." 1 John 1:8 reminds us that we all sin. Most of us practice sinning some of the time. How do we reconcile this with 1 John 3:9? In Romans 7:17 and 20, Paul explains that when he sinned, it was not I (the new man), but sin that dwelt within him (the old man). In Ephesians 4:22-24, we are told to put off the old man and put on the new man which is the same as walking not after the flesh, but after the spirit (Romans 8:4) and walking in the light, not in darkness (Romans 1:6-7).

I believe that to suggest or imply that the new spiritual man who is born of the Spirit of God can sin, but cannot practice sin, is at least an insult to the Holy Spirit and, at worst, blasphemy.

The Matter of Forgiving

> *We must forgive others even as God for Christ's sake forgave us. Does this not mean that we must forgive unconditionally?* (Ephesians 4:32)

No. God does not forgive unconditionally. I can only find one account in the Bible of anyone forgiving anybody unconditionally. That is Eli. He is a clear example of the seriousness of forgiving unconditionally. (1 Samuel 2:12-22 and 3:13-14)

God makes allowance for those who do not know what they are doing. (Leviticus 4:13-14) If the congregation, ruler, or anyone of the common people sinned in ignorance, they were not held accountable until they knew they had sinned. (Leviticus 4:22-23 and 27-28)

God did not hold Eli accountable until Eli knew what his sons were doing. When Eli honoured his sons above God, God did not forgive him. Eli had to bear his iniquity. (1 Samuel 2:22, 27-36 and 3:11-14)

In Luke 23:34, Jesus forgave his enemies. Why? Because of their ignorance. Acts 3:17 confirms that they acted in ignorance.

Stephen did the same for his enemies in Acts 7:58-60. Paul was one of them. In 1 Timothy 1:12-13, Paul says, "I obtained mercy, because I did it ignorantly in unbelief."

Acts 20:20-21 says that people who know they have done wrong must repent to be forgiven. That is the message Jesus gave His disciples to teach (Luke 24:46–47) and the message Peter taught (Acts 2:38 and Acts 3:19).

When Moses and Aaron rebelled (Numbers 20:7-12 and Numbers 24) and did not repent, they were not forgiven. They had to bear their iniquity. (Numbers 27:12-14)

These principles are confirmed by the parable of the two debtors in Matthew 18:23-35. The first pleaded for mercy, promised to pay (repentance), and was forgiven. The second pleaded for mercy, promised to pay, and should have been forgiven.

Joseph wanted to forgive his brothers, but held out until he was sure they had repented. Then there was an honest and joyful reconciliation. (Genesis 42:21-24 and chapters 44 and 45).

If a brother trespasses against another brother, the Lord's command is crystal clear. Repentance is a condition for forgiving known sin. (Luke 17:3-4 and Matthew 18:15-17) The doctrine of unconditional forgiving is a flagrant violation of this commandment. If we are bitter and vengeful, it is not because we will not forgive someone who God will not forgive. It is because we do not love that person, as we are commanded to do.

> *This is my commandment that ye love one another as I have loved you.* (John 15:12)

Love your enemies, bless them that curse you, do good to them that hate you, and pray for them which despitefully use you and persecute you. (Matthew 5:44)

As light dispels the darkness, of the darkest night, So love dispels the darkness, of bitterness and spite.

God does not forgive us because He loves us. He forgives us when, as repentant sinners, we believe what He has done to save us. Because He loved us, He suffered and rose from the dead the third day. Therefore, repentance and remission of sins should be preached in His name among all nations. (Luke 24:46-47 and 2 Peter 3:9).

Paul taught from house to house testifying to both Jews and Greeks repentance towards God and faith towards our Lord Jesus Christ. (Acts 20:21)

> *If we confess our sins [repentance], He is faithful and just to forgive us our sins, and to cleanse us from all unrighteousness.* (1 John 1:9)

In Ephesians 4:30, it says that we, in turn, are to forgive others (when they repent) even as God for Christ's sake has forgiven us (when we repented).

That is the message found in the following:

> *Take heed to yourselves: if thy brother trespass against thee, rebuke him; and if he repent, forgive him. And if he trespass against thee seven times in a day, and seven times in a day turn again to thee, saying, I repent [and means it]; thou shalt forgive him.* (Luke 17:3-4)

Suppose a brother steals your ATV, and you confront him about it. He admits his guilt and returns it, and offers compensation for any damages [repentance]. He can now be absolved from blame [forgiven]. Fellowship is restored, and there is an honest reconciliation. Furthermore, God will forgive him, and you have saved him from the vengeance of God coming upon him as promised in (1 Thessalonians 4:6):

Let no man go beyond and defraud his brother in any matter, for the Lord is the avenger of all such as we have forewarned you and testified.

If he will not return the ATV, we know that he has not repented. If we love him, we will do all we can to convince him to repent as in Matthew 18: 15 to 17). If he hungers, feed him. If he thirsts, give him drink (Romans 12: 20), but he must not be given any reason to believe he can be forgiven by God or man if he does not repent. (Hebrews 10: 26: 32)

> The following story illustrates how this tradition of unconditional forgiving is completely devoid of common sense and compassion, and is contrary to the inborn sense of right and wrong that is written in the hearts of all mankind (Romans 2:14–15) It is also an outright contradiction of (Luke 17:3–4) and (Matthew 18:15–17)

Forgive and Forget?
Dear *Grainews*:

I read with great interest, admiration, and respect and with tears, the letter from Mr. John Kapicki, "Forgive me …" (*Grainews*, December, page 11). I agree wholeheartedly with Mr. Kapicki and respect him because he is the only person who has had the guts to write and stand up to the clergy, be it pastors, reverends or priests, and say, "Enough is enough." It's easy to stand in a pulpit and quote, "Forgive and forget," but have they ever had to practice it in their lives?

I'd like to tell you a story and, when you are through reading it, perhaps you will agree "forgive and forget" does not exist when it comes to hurting, nightmares, scars on your body and, even more important, scars on your heart which never heal.

I am in my mid-50s, born and raised in a large city, the youngest of a large Roman Catholic family, dirt poor, but well educated, good, warm, loving people.

I was only six days into my 12th year. One night, I had gone skating at our local park and my older brother was to pick me up at 8 p.m. He had a date and asked my other brother to do him a favor.

Unfortunately, this other brother was busy playing hockey with friends and forgot about his little sister. I waited for awhile and decided to walk home alone. It was close by and I felt safe. A car pulled up to ask for directions, and I noticed it had an American license plate. Forgetting the advice of my parents, I approached the car to give them the proper directions when the back door opened and I was pulled in. Before the blow of a pipe hit my head, I noticed there were three men.

Several hours later, I was found in an alley, a block and a half away from home, a cold winter night, 40 below zero, a 12-year-old child lying in a pool of blood, stark naked, head split open, face all beaten, breast slashed, raped, and many bones broken, including hands, feet, and pelvis.

I awoke a few days later and saw my mother sitting by my bed crying, with her beads in her hands, and my father sobbing. Looking at them both, I remember saying, "I love you, please don't cry. Tell me what happened and why I am in so much pain."

They explained what had happened. I was in a body cast from head to foot, not one inch of my body was visible except for my face, which was swollen to twice its size, with two black eyes. Being a tiny, delicate, innocent little girl, I couldn't comprehend why anyone would do such a thing. I had never hurt anyone. Needless to say, I cried and cried, not so much from the pain of my body, but the pain in my heart.

I was still in the hospital when I turned 13, after several surgeries and new casts. I spent the whole year determined I would walk out in the same condition I was in before this horrific nightmare began. From 13 to 14, I was in therapy for my limbs, and in therapy to help me overcome my fear of men.

My parents, God bless them, gave me strength and encouragement even though I could see the pain in their faces as they recalled how good natured I was previously – always smiling, laughing, singing, and dancing. All they could see in me now was anger. So they understood when I told them I was no longer a child, but a woman and wanted to start working.

With their permission, I started a job in a financial office full time, held down two part-time jobs, completed and received my diploma for grade 12 from night school, and successfully completed two years of business college. My attitude was, I would prove to the world how strong I was even though total strangers had tried to kill me. God saved me for a reason. With head held high, my self worth, pride, and dignity, I made something of my life. But there was more grief to come.

My two older brothers blamed themselves and became alcoholics for years. Eventually, my attitude rubbed off on them and they turned out to be great husbands and fathers.

At 16, the doctors advised me the damage to my lower body was so severe, I would never bear a child – another blow and scar on my heart. All my family had children, and in those days the belief was, "You were not a complete woman unless you had a child."

I hid my tears and accepted what the doctors told me, but I couldn't believe it.

At 17, I married a very gentle young man and, sure enough, a few months later I was expecting and very, very happy, even though I had to spend five months in bed. I was going to have a child and prove the medical profession wrong. I could do it.

Towards the end of the seventh month, my son was stillborn. More tears and another scar on my heart. The following year, I was back in the hospital. This time, it was a tubal pregnancy. The ovary and tube on the right side had burst. Immediate surgery was required or I wouldn't have made it. I didn't care at this point, but it meant only more tears and more scars.

My husband turned cold toward me and, before I reached the ripe old age of 20, he left me for another woman. We divorced – his reason for leaving me: "I want someone who will bear me children." Once again, tears and more scars.

When I reached 21, I had to have a full hysterectomy. I cried for three solid days, begging the doctors not to take away my only hope of at least one more chance of having a child of my own. My pleas were fruitless. It was surgery or die.

I was baptized, confirmed, had first communion, solemn communion, and married, all by the same priest. After my surgery at 21, being a faithful Catholic, I returned to church for my Friday confession to receive communion on Sunday. My big sin to confess was I had wished ill health on my attackers. This priest, who knew me all my life and preached to me from 12 to 21 to "forgive and forget," refused me absolution. The reason was, not only was I excommunicated from my religion for having been divorced, I would also need proof of my surgery.

Throughout all my tears and scars, I learned over the years to hide my pain, anger and bitterness, except when I hear those infamous words being quoted – "Forgive and forget." I can never forgive anyone for ruining my life, stealing my teenage years, nor can I ever forget all the pain over the years – the nightmares, fear of the dark, a son I never got to hold. Every day, I think of him. How can you forget when you're bathing and see the scars – a constant reminder of insidious human beings who got away with it?

My dad died of a broken heart when I was 17, and my mother's hair was white by the time I was 21. I will never, never forgive, and I cannot forget.

The Bible says: "Repent and you shall be forgiven." If those three men were forgiven of a horrible crime, I wonder to whom they repented. Certainly not to me. Therefore why should I be constantly told to "forgive and forget"?

Every time I held one of nieces or nephews in my arms, I would quote with silent tears the words, "How can I forgive and forget? You could have been mine."

—Name withheld
Printed by permission

No Condemnation

There is therefore now no condemnation to them which are in Christ Jesus, who walk not after the flesh, but after the Spirit. (Romans 8:1)

Does this mean that no Christian can ever be condemned? (Romans 8:1)

Yes and no, depending on the Greek word that is used: ***krisis***, ***krima*** or ***katakrima*** (according to *Strong's Concordance*).

Krisis – This condemnation is the Lake of Fire – the punishment for rejecting Christ. (John 3:19 and John 5:24)

Krima – This condemnation is physical death, the due reward for the wrong they were believed to have done. (Luke 23:40-41)

Katakrima – This condemnation is literal or figurative death that is the result of a Christian being carnally minded and living after the flesh and not after the Spirit. (Romans 8:4-7, 13).

Christ is the vine, and believers are the branches. Abiding in Him is more than just being saved and becoming a branch. Abiding is the same as walking in the Spirit and walking in the light. Some branches in Him do not produce the fruit of the Spirit because they do not abide in Him. They have chosen to live after the flesh and not after the Spirit. (John 15:1-11).

Ananias and Sapphira are examples of "branches in Him", who chose to sin willfully and were condemned to premature physical death. (John 15:2 and Acts 5) 1 Corinthians 10:1-12 gives examples of thousands, as well as Eli, Gehazi, Moses, and Aaron, who were condemned to premature death for willful sin. 1 Timothy 5:24 and 2 Timothy 4:1 tell of some whose sins were open and condemned beforehand.

Willful sin, not judged in this life, will be judged and condemned at His appearing and His kingdom at the judgment seat of Christ. (Matthew 19:27-30 and 2 Corinthians 5:10-11a)

In conclusion, they will receive appropriate punishment (condemnation) for the wrong they have done and the account will be settled. (Matthew 24:48-51, Matthew 25:24-30, Luke 12:45-48, 1 Corinthians 3:17, Colossians 3:25, Galatians 6:7, Hebrews 10:26-31)

Willful Sin

> *For if we sin willfully after that we have received the knowledge of the truth, there remaineth no more sacrifice for sins.* (Hebrews 10:26)

Is "willful sin" found in Hebrews 10:26 the same as rejecting Christ?

No. The context of Hebrews 10:26 clearly establishes that those who sin willfully are the people of God. They cannot reject Christ or be lost because they have been purchased by Him and are sealed until the day of redemption. (Ephesians 1:13-14) It cannot be said of non-Christians that they "count the blood of the covenant wherewith they were sanctified an unholy thing". (Hebrews 10:29) Nor does God ever say of those who reject Him that they are His people. (Hebrews 10:30)

Not all sins are willful. People are not accountable for sins committed in ignorance. The principles regarding sin are the same in the Old Testament as in the New. Sin is not imputed when there is no law (Romans 5:13).

> *Father, forgive them; for they know not what they do.* (Luke 23:34)

> *I know that through ignorance ye did it, as did also your rulers.* (Acts 3:17)

> *... But I obtained mercy, because I did it ignorantly and in unbelief.* (1 Timothy 1:13)

When the sin of ignorance becomes known, then they were told to repent, make confession and be forgiven. (Leviticus 4:14, 23, 28 and Acts 3:14-19)

Likewise, sins committed in the weakness of the flesh are not necessarily willful; they can be confessed, repented of, and forgiven (if their repentence is genuine) (2 Samuel 12:13-14).

> *Let the wicked forsake his way, and the unrighteous man his thoughts: and let him return unto the Lord, and he will have mercy upon him; and to our God, for He will abundantly pardon.* (Isaiah 55:7)

> *If we confess our sins, He is faithful and just to forgive us our sins, and to cleanse us from all unrighteousness.* (1 John 1:9)

Sometimes the people of God commit sin in the weakness of the flesh as David did, and do not confess or repent of it until after they are caught. However, because what they did was not done as an act of defiance (presumptuous or willful), they were spared from the death penalty, but were still punished according to the sin they committed. Other examples of this are:

Miriam (Numbers 12): Seemingly, out of envy of Moses' authority, she stirred up Aaron against him and faulted him for the woman he married. Because she did not die for her sin, it could not have been willful, but she was punished according to her deed by being made a leper as white as snow and was kept outside the camp for seven days. The account was then settled.

Gehazi (2 Kings 5:27): Gehazi did not die for taking a gift from Naaman, so it was not a willful sin, but he was punished according to his deed by having the leprosy of Naaman on himself and on his seed forever. Then the account was settled.

What is willful sin?

Willful sin is sin that is committed as an act of defiance toward God. Such sins are called:

- Presumptuous
- Rebellion
- Willful
- Falling away
- Despising the word of the Lord
- Counting the blood of the covenant wherewith we were sanctified an unholy thing

God will not grant repentance or accept a confession for willful sin. The perpetrators must bear their iniquity, and the punishment is death.

> *But if a man come presumptuously upon his neighbor, to slay him with guile; thou shalt take him from mine altar, that he may die.* (Exodus 21:14)

> *But the soul that doeth ought presumptuously … and that soul shall be cut off from among his people. Because he hath despised the word of the Lord, and has broken His*

> *commandment, that soul shall utterly be cut off; his iniquity shall be upon him.* (Numbers 15:30-31)

> *And the man that will do presumptuously, and will not hearken unto the priest that standeth to minister there before the Lord thy God, or unto the judge, even that man shall die: and thou shalt put away the evil from Israel. And all the people shall hear, and fear, and do no more presumptuously.* (Deuteronomy 17:12-13)

Some examples are:

- All 603,548 men of war who rebelled at Kadesh died prematurely and never got into the Promised Land. (Numbers 1:46, 14:4-10, 29, 26:64-65)
- The man who "despised the word of the Lord" gathered sticks on the Sabbath. (Numbers 15:32-36)
- Eli, who honoured his sons above God, was assured that none of his seed would die of old age, and he and his two sons died prematurely. (1 Samuel 2:12-34, 3:14, 4:10-18)
- Ananias and Sapphira died for willful (presumptuous) sin. (Acts 5:1-11)
- Some who ate and drank unworthily (presumptuously) died. (1 Corinthians 11:29-32).
- Thousands of the "people of God" who "fell" died in the wilderness because of presumptuous sin are listed in the New Testament as examples to us to not fall as they did. (1 Corinthians 10:1-12)

This warning about falling is confirmed in Hebrews 3:8-19, Hebrews 4:1, Hebrews 4:11, Hebrews 6:4-6, and Hebrews 10:26-31.

Even Moses and Aaron committed one act of rebellion (Numbers 27:12 –14) and paid the price by dying prematurely, and did not get to enter the Promised Land. There was no water for the congregation, and they blamed Moses and Aaron. (Numbers 20:2)

> *And Moses and Aaron went away from presence of the assembly unto the door of the tabernacle of the congregation, and fell upon their faces: and the glory of the Lord appeared unto them. And the Lord spake unto Moses saying, Take the rod, and gather thou the assembly together, thou, and Aaron*

> *thy brother, and speak ye unto the rock before their eyes; and it shall give forth his water …* (Numbers 20:6-8)

> *And Moses and Aaron gathered the congregation together before the rock, and he said unto them, Hear now, ye rebels; must we fetch you water out of this rock? And Moses lifted up his hand, and with his rod he smote the rock twice: and the water came out abundantly, and the congregation drank, and their beasts also. And the Lord spake unto Moses and Aaron, Because ye believed me not, to sanctify me in the eyes of the children of Israel, therefore ye shall not bring this congregation into the land which I have given them.* (Numbers 20:10-12)

> *And the Lord spake unto Moses and Aaron … for he shall not enter into the land which I have given unto the children of Israel, because ye rebelled against my word at the water of Meribah.* (Numbers 20:23-24)

> *And Aaron the priest went up into mount Hor … and died there, in the fortieth year after the children of Israel were come out of the land of Egypt, in the first day of the fifth month.* (Numbers 33:38)

> *And the Lord said unto Moses, Get thee up into this mount Abarim, and see the land which I have given to the children of Israel … thou shalt be gathered unto thy people, as Aaron thy brother was gathered. For ye rebelled against my commandment in the desert of Zin, in the strife of the congregation, to sanctify me at the water before their eyes* … (Numbers 27:12-14)

Moses died in the fortieth year in the eleventh month, and I believe the account was settled in full. (Deuteronomy 1:3)

> *There arose not a prophet since in Israel like unto Moses, whom the Lord knew face to face.* (Deuteronomy 34:10)

Outer Darkness

Is "outer darkness" another term for the "lake of fire"?

No. Outer darkness is found only three times in the New Testament. Each time it is a reference to the Judgment Seat of Christ for deeds done in the body that are bad. (2 Corinthians 5:10-11a)

Some children of the kingdom will be "cast into outer darkness". There will be weeping and gnashing of teeth. (Matthew 8:12) Compare the following:

- Some will be saved yet though as by fire. (1 Corinthians 3:15)
- They will not have any inheritance in His millennial kingdom. (1 Corinthians 6:9-10 and Ephesians 5:5)
- The vengeance of God will come to a "brother" who defrauds a brother. (1 Thessalonians 4:6)

The man referred to in Matthew 22:13, is cast into "outer darkness" because the wedding garments are the righteous acts of the saints, Revelation 19:8; and he was a "branch in Him" that had not produced material for a wedding dress, John 15:2. An inheritance in His kingdom is for those who earn it. (Colossians 3:23-24) Any who do wrong (and do not repent) will be punished accordingly. (Colossians 3:25)

The servant who buried his talent was cast into "outer darkness". (Matthew 25:30)

Other forms of punishment for unfaithful servants are:

- Saved yet so as by fire (1 Corinthians 3:15)
- Destroyed (1 Corinthians 3:16-17)
- Beaten with many or few stripes (Luke 12:27-28)
- Having their portion with the hypocrites (Matthew 24:51)
- Having no inheritance in the kingdom (1 Corinthians 6:8-10)

In conclusion, "outer darkness" is one form of punishment for "willful sin" on the part of the people of God. People who go to the lake of fire for rejecting Christ are not at this judgment. They are not resurrected until the 1,000 years are ended. (2 Corinthians 5:10-11a and Revelation 20:5)

Falling Away

For it is impossible for those who were once enlightened, and have tasted of the heavenly gift, and were made partakers of the Holy Ghost, and have tasted the good word of God, and the powers of the world to come, if they shall fall away, to renew them again unto repentance; seeing they crucify to themselves the Son of God afresh, and put him to an open shame. (Hebrews 6:4-6)

Is "falling away" the same as rejecting Christ? (Hebrews 6:4-6)

No. The context of this passage is addressed to believers who are said to be sanctified and made partakers of the Holy Ghost, and are referred to as:

- We (Hebrews 2:1, 4:3, 4:14-15, 6:3)
- Us (Hebrews 4:1, 4:6, 4:11, 6:1)
- Brethren (Hebrews 2:11, 3:12)
- Holy Brethren (Hebrews 3:1)

We believers are exhorted to:

- Give earnest heed (Hebrews 2:1)
- Not neglect (Hebrews 2:3)
- Believe (Hebrews 3:18-19)
- Fear (Hebrews 4:1)
- Hold fast (Hebrews 10:23)
- Exhort (Hebrews 10:25)

All this, so that we as believers will not:

- Slip (Hebrews 2:1)
- Harden our hearts (Hebrews 3:8)
- Depart from the living God (Hebrews 3:12)
- Fail to enter his "rest" (Hebrews 4:1) (the millennium)
- Come short (Hebrews 4:1)

- Fall (1 Corinthians 10:1-12)
- Fall away (Hebrews 6:4)
- Sin willfully (Hebrews 10:26)

If we fall as they fell, we will be worthy of greater punishment. (Hebrews 10:27-30) This punishment is being nigh unto cursing whose end is to be burned. (Hebrews 6:8) Nigh unto cursing and being burned is not the lake of fire. I believe it is comparable to being saved, yet so as by fire. (1 Corinthians 3:15)

Let us serve God acceptably with reverence and godly fear, for our God is a consuming fire. (Hebrews 12:28-29) Believers cannot be lost, but they can fall just as the 603,548 men of war fell, and Eli, Miriam, Aaron, and Moses fell. (1 Corinthians 10:1-12) Falling away is trampling Him underfoot – counting the blood of the covenant whereby we were sanctified an unholy thing (Hebrews 10:29), doing despite unto the Spirit of grace, sinning willfully.

In conclusion, because the context of all of the above terms are definitely addressed to believers, those who fall are not rejecting Christ. If Moses fell, anybody can fall and will have to bear their iniquity either in this life as Moses and Aaron (Numbers 20:12 and 24, 27:12-14) and as Ananias and Sapphira did (Acts 5), or during the millennium (1 Timothy 5:24 and Colossians 3:25).

Terror

> *Knowing therefore the terror of the Lord, we persuade men; but we are made manifest unto God …* (2 Corinthians 5:11a)

What is meant by the word "terror" in 2 Corinthians 5:11a?

According to *Strong's Concordance*, the Greek word *phobos* means alarm or fright. I do not believe there is any other valid definition.

The unprofitable servant was cast into outer (terrifying) darkness. (Matthew 25:30).

Paul exercised self-control so he would not be a castaway (1 Corinthians 9:27). He laboured to be accepted of Him so as to avoid the terror of the Lord. He faithfully warned us in all of his epistles (2 Corinthians 5:9-11a). We must warn the righteous not to turn from his righteousness (Ezekiel 3:20-21).

Jesus warns us about being faithful and not being unfaithful. (Matthew 24:44-51) He also warns us to not let our lights go out (Matthew 25:1-13) and to be careful about what we do with our talents (Matthew 25:13-20).

Peter warns us to respect the cost of our redemption (1 Peter 1:17-19), and to diligently seek an abundant entrance to His kingdom (the Millennial Kingdom) (2 Peter 1:10-11).

We are warned by John not to lose out on a full reward (1 John 2:28).

Hebrews 9:27 warns of the certainty of the judgment. Hebrews 3:12-19 warns about not entering His "rest" (the millennial kingdom). Hebrews 4:1-11 warns about coming short of it. We are warned about the awful consequences of willful sin in Hebrews 10:23-31. Hebrews 12:15-29, Ephesians 5:5, and (1 Corinthians 6:1–20) warn of losing our inheritance in the kingdom.

In conclusion, if every Christian is not "afraid" of falling, they should be – just as God told Miriam that she should have been afraid to speak against His servant Moses. (Numbers 12:8)

Good Friday and the Crucifixion

Wednesday 14th		Thursday 15th		Friday 16th		Saturday 17th		Sunday 18th	
DAY		DAY		DAY		DAY		DAY	
Crucified	BURIED	Leviticus 23:6; Sabbath of unleavened bread				Weekly Sabbath	empty tomb		
	NIGHT		NIGHT		NIGHT		NIGHT		NIGHT

Christians the world over accept and teach that Jesus was crucified on Friday, and the tomb was empty sometime before daylight on Sunday. How can you question what theologians have concluded for 2,000 years? (John 20:1)

Jesus promised that a sign proving His deity would be that He would be three days and three nights in the heart of the earth. (Matthew 12:39-40) It is not possible for that length of time to equal three days and three nights – not even parts of days and parts of nights.

Some claim that by Jewish reckoning, any part of a day is regarded as a whole day. I do not know of any historical or biblical evidence of such reckoning by Jews or any other nation. Even Joshua's long day is not referred to as a whole day. (Joshua 10:13) Also in the days of Hezekiah, there is no hint that the forty minutes on the dial of Ahaz was equivalent to a whole day. (2 Kings 20:11)

We know that Joseph did not get the body until the evening (Matthew 27:57), and that by the time they had prepared his body for burial (as the manner of the Jews is to bury), it would have been well after dark. (John 19:39- 40) We also know that the tomb was empty before daylight Sunday morning.

> *The first day of the week cometh Mary Magdalene early when it was yet dark unto the sepulcher and seeth the stone taken away from the sepulchre.* (John 20:1)

Therefore, we know that he was in the grave for one day and parts of two nights ... if he was crucified on Friday.

One of those two nights had to be part of Saturday, and the other night had to be part of either Friday or Sunday. It cannot be both. We have to conclude that the time in the grave, according to so-called Jewish reckoning, could not have been more than two 24-hour days. Calling it three days is mathematically impossible.

In Matthew 12:39-40, Jesus said that keeping this promise would be the only sign He would give to prove that He was who He claimed to be. In John 11:9, He said, "Are there not 12 hours in a day?" This shows that when He spoke of days and nights, He meant 12-hour days and 12-hour nights. Mark 15:42 and John 19:14 tell us that the day He was crucified was the same day as the Passover, and that the next day was a "high day" (a Sabbath).

I believe tradition errs in assuming that, that Sabbath was the seventh day of the week.

Exodus 12:5-6 says that the Passover lamb was always killed on the 14th day of the month. They not only prepared for Passover, but they also had to get ready so they would not have to do any work the next day (the 15th day). The 14th was the preparation day. The next day (the 15th day) was the first day of the "feast of unleavened bread". It was a Sabbath, a holy convocation, so no servile work could be done on that day (Leviticus 23:5-8).

John 19:31 says that the Sabbath of Unleavened Bread was called a high day, distinguishing it from the weekly Sabbath. Teaching that Christ was crucified on Friday makes him a false prophet because He did not deliver on the sign that He said would prove that He was the Christ. (Deuteronomy 18:21-22, Matthew 12:39-40, Matthew 27:21-22, Matthew 27:63-66, Mark 8:31, and John 2:19). The year Jesus was crucified, the 14th day of the month would have been on a Wednesday, and He kept his promise exactly as He had said.

This is the time line I believe: He was already hanging on the cross by noon, the sixth hour of the day. He died at 3:00 p.m. His friends removed Him from the cross some time before 6:00 p.m. He could have been entombed at any time before midnight. He would have risen from the tomb 72 hours later. The empty tomb was discovered sometime before daylight on Sunday morning.

In conclusion, in the year that Christ was crucified, the 14th day was a Wednesday, and Jesus kept his promise by doing exactly as He said He would do.

CHAPTER FOUR
A Summation Of Three Long Standing Traditions

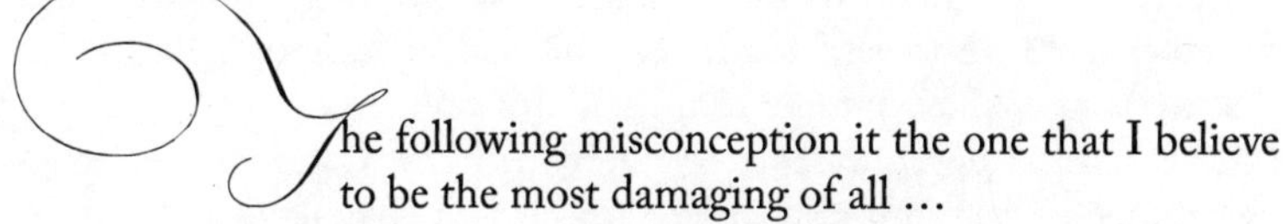

he following misconception it the one that I believe to be the most damaging of all …

Tradition #1: God Forgives Unconditionally and We Must Do as He Does

This tradition does not stand the test of Scripture. Examples sometimes given are:

> *Then said Jesus, Father, forgive them; for they know not what they do.* (Luke 23:32)

> *And be ye kind one to another, tenderhearted, forgiving one another, even as God for Christ's sake hath forgiven you.* (Ephesians 4:32)

The quote from Luke is not unconditional. The condition is that they do not know what they are doing. Acts 3:15-18 confirms that they had killed the Prince of Life because they did it in ignorance as did their rulers. After the resurrection, they knew they had been wrong and were told to repent in order for their sins to be blotted out. Likewise, Paul testifies in 1 Timothy 1:13 that he "was before a blasphemer, and a persecutor, and injurious: but I obtained mercy, because I did it ignorantly in unbelief."

God does not forgive unconditionally. When one knows he has sinned, he must repent to be forgiven.

> … *Except ye repent, ye shall all likewise perish.* (Luke 13:3)

> … *Thus it is written, and thus it behooved Christ to suffer, and to rise from the dead the third day: and that repentance and remission of sins should be preached in his name among all nations* … (Luke 24:46-47)

> *And the times of this ignorance God winked at: but now commandeth all men every where to repent.* (Acts 17:30)

> *The Lord is … not willing that any should perish, but that all should come to repentance.* (2 Peter 3:9)

Some might say that according to John 3:15, Jesus did not tell Nicodemus to repent. That is because Nicodemus had already confessed repentance toward God when he said in John 3:2, "We know that thou are a teacher come from God: for no man can do these miracles that thou doest, except God be with him." Likewise, Cornelius and the Jailer were not told to repent as it was obvious that they were already repentant toward God in accordance with Acts 20:21 where Paul testified "both to the Jews, and also to the Greeks, repentance toward God, and faith toward our Lord Jesus Christ."

With regard to the earlier-quoted Ephesians 4:32, many interpret this verse to mean that God forgives unconditionally and, therefore, so must we. God did not forgive us unconditionally. He forgave us for Christ's sake when we repented. (Luke 24:46-47) We must forgive others when they repent, just as he forgave us when we repented.

> *Take heed to yourselves: If thy brother trespass against thee, rebuke him; and if he repent, forgive him.* (Luke 17:3)

Matthew 18:15-17 states that if the last effort to get him to repent fails, then "let him be unto thee as a heathen man and a publican" (someone to love, someone who needs to repent to be forgiven). Bitterness can be overcome by unconditional love. Unconditional love will withhold forgiveness for his sake until he repents. Unconditional forgiveness is unbiblical – a violation of a commandment of the Lord.

God is a holy God. He cannot forgive one who knows he has done wrong and will not repent.

Tradition #2: Christians Have Nothing to Fear

This tradition is only true when Christians are walking in the Spirit.

> *This I say then, Walk in the Spirit, and ye shall not fulfill the lust of the flesh.* (Galatians 5:16)

It is not true of Christians who are living after the flesh as some Christians in Corinth were doing and as some Christians are doing today.

It is God who introduced the fear factor to his people.

> *And the man that will do presumptuously … even that man shall die: and thou shalt put away the evil from Israel.*

> *And all the people shall hear, and fear, and do no more presumptuously.* (Deuteronomy 17:12-13)

> *… Fear God, and keep his commandments: for this is the whole duty of man. For God shall bring every work into judgment, with every secret thing, whether it be good, or whether it be evil.* (Ecclesiastes 12:13-14)

> *Wherefore we labour, that, whether present or absent, we may be accepted of him. For we must all appear before the judgment seat of Christ: that every one may receive the things done in his body, according to that he hath done, whether it be good or bad. Knowing therefore the terror of the Lord, we persuade men …* (2 Corinthians 5:9-11a)

> *Some men's sins are open beforehand, going before to judgment; and some men they follow after.* (1 Timothy 5:24)

> *He that despised Moses' law died without mercy under two or three witnesses: of how much sorer punishment, suppose ye, shall he be thought worthy, who hath trodden under foot the Son of God, and hath counted the blood of the covenant, wherewith he was sanctified, an unholy thing, and hath done despite unto the Spirit of grace? For we know him that hath said, Vengeance belongeth unto me, I will recompense, saith the Lord. And again, The Lord shall judge His people. It is a fearful thing to fall unto the hands of the living God.* (Hebrews 10:28-31)

> *And if ye call on the Father, who without respect of persons judgeth according to every man's work, pass the time of your sojourning here in fear …* (1 Peter 1:17-19)

We are given many examples of some of the people of God who would not repent of the wrong they had done and were judged beforehand. Some of these are:

- The 603,548 men of war who rebelled against God, died in the wilderness and never got to the Promised Land. (Numbers 14:10, 29-30, 26:51, 63-64)
- The man who should have been afraid to despise the word of the Lord (Numbers 15:30-36).

- Korah should have been afraid to rebel and was swallowed by the earth. (Numbers 16:1-32)
- Gehazi should have been "afraid" to do what he knew was wrong. (2 Kings 5:20–27)
- Achan should have been afraid to sin presumptuously. (Numbers 15:30-31 and Joshua 7:24-26).
- Uzziah should have been afraid to burn incense (2 Chronicles 26:14-20).
- 23,000 of the people of God should have been afraid to commit fornication (1 Corinthians 10:1-12) and are said to be examples to us to not fall as they fell (Hebrews 4:11).
- Ananias and Sapphira should have been afraid to lie to God. They died prematurely and great fear came upon all the church and those who heard what had happened (Acts 5:1-11).
- Some who should have been afraid to eat and drink unworthily (1 Corinthians 11:30-31).
- Aaron should have been afraid to rebel against the Lord (Numbers 27:12-14).
- Likewise, Moses should have been afraid to rebel against the Lord (Numbers 27:12-14).
- Miriam should have been afraid to speak against Moses (Numbers 12:1-15).
- Moses, Aaron and Miriam remind us that even devout servants of God need to be on their guard against falling away.

> *Wherefore the rather, brethren, give diligence to make your calling and election sure: for if ye do these things, ye shall never fall.* (2 Peter 1:10)

God has given us four incentives to serve him and to guard us from falling away (Hebrews 4:11):

- Love

> *For the love of Christ constraineth us ...*
> (2 Corinthians 5:14)

- Duty

... for necessity is laid upon me ... (1 Corinthians 9:16)

- Reward

... willingly, I have a reward ... (1 Corinthians 9:17)

- Fear

... Woe is unto me, if I preach not the gospel! (1 Corinthians 9:16)

Knowing therefore the terror of the Lord, we persuade men. (2 Corinthians 5:11)

Fear the Lord, and depart from evil. (Proverbs 3:7)

[God said to Miriam] Wherefore then were ye not afraid to speak against my servant Moses? (Numbers 12:8)

How sad that there were so many who were not afraid to do what they did. Some commentators insist that fear does not mean to be afraid; that it is better translated as "reverential trust". That would make 1 John 4:18 read, "There is no *reverential trust* in love; but perfect love casteth out *reverential trust* because *reverential trust* has torment. He that has *reverential trust* is not made perfect in love."

On the judgment day of 2 Corinthians 5:10, *will the Lord say to the carnal Christians*:

Did you not know that your body is the temple of the Holy Ghost which is in you, which ye have of God, and ye are not your own? For you are bought with a price: therefore glorify God in your body, and in your spirit, which are God's. (1 Corinthians 6:19-20)

Know ye not that ye are the temple of God, and that the Spirit of God dwelleth in you? If any man defile the temple of God, him shall God destroy; for the temple of God is holy, which temple ye are. (1 Corinthians 3:16-17)

And will they answer? Our churches have assured us, over and over, that we have nothing to fear. They teach us that "there is no condemnation to them that are in Christ Jesus".

This quotation from the first verse of Romans chapter 8; is a contradiction of the rest of the chapter 8; (which is the context of verse one). It also contradicts Matthew 24:48-51, Colossians 3:25, and Ezekiel 3:20, 1 Peter 1:17–19.

Tradition #3: God Cannot Punish a Christian Because All of his Sins Were Covered at the Cross

This is true in the sense that in the eyes of the Father the righteousness of Christ has been imputed to every believer. Ephesians 1:13-14 says in part, "In whom also after that ye believed, ye were sealed with that Holy Spirit of promise … until the redemption of the purchased possession." For this reason, the Father will judge no man, but has committed all judgment to the Son. (John 5:22) Salvation is never at stake. It is guaranteed until the day of redemption. The judgment seat of Christ (2 Corinthians 5:10-11a) is to determine what those who are saved will receive for the deeds done in the body since they were saved, whether they be good or bad. The Father has committed all judgment to the Son, who will judge when He comes. (John 5:27)

> *For the Son of man shall come in the glory of his Father with his angels; and then he shall reward every man according to his works.* (Matthew 16:27)

In Revelation 20:4b, the martyrs of the tribulation will be rewarded by reigning with Him for 1,000 years.

To say there is no punishment at this judgment is not true.

The Son is the judge.

> *And hath given him authority to execute judgment also, because he is the Son of man.* (John 5:27)

Paul laboured to be rewarded and not punished at that judgment (2 Corinthians 5:9-11) and not to be a castaway (1 Corinthians 9:27). John warned us not to have to be ashamed (1 John 2:28) and to strive for a full reward (2 John 8). Peter warns us of that judgment also. (1 Peter 1:17-19) Likewise Paul warns us.

> *But he that doeth wrong shall receive for the wrong which he hath done: there is no respect of persons.* (Colossians 3:25)

> *He that despised Moses' law died without mercy under two or three witnesses: of how much sorer punishment, suppose ye, shall he be thought worthy, who hath trodden under foot*

> *the Son of God, and hath counted the blood of the covenant, wherewith he was sanctified, an unholy thing, and hath done despite unto the Spirit of grace? For we know him that hath said, Vengeance belongeth unto me, I will recompense, saith the Lord. And again, The Lord shall judge his people. It is a fearful thing to fall into the hands of the living God.* (Hebrews 10:28-31)

> *If ye call on the Father, who without respect of persons judgeth according to every man's work, pass the time of your sojourning here in fear: Forasmuch as ye know that ye were not redeemed with corruptible things, as silver and gold, from your vain conversation received by tradition from your fathers; but with the precious blood of Christ as of a lamb without blemish and without spot.* (1 Peter 1:17-19)

Concerning that judgment, Jesus said that faithful servants will be rewarded (Matthew 24:44-47 and unfaithful servants will be punished (Matthew 24:48-51). Again, in Matthew 25:13-23, faithful servants will be rewarded by ruling with Him. The servant who buried his talent will be punished causing weeping and gnashing of teeth. (Note that this judgment is at the time of the first resurrection of Revelation 20:4 when His 1,000-year reign begins.) There are no unbelievers at this judgment because they are not resurrected until the 1,000 years are finished.

> *But the rest of the dead lived not again until the thousand years were finished. This is the first resurrection.* (Revelation 20:5)

Therefore, we have to conclude that the unfaithful servants are carnal Christians who are "saved yet so as by fire" (1 Corinthians 3:15).

During the 1000 years, all the saints will have been fully recompensed for the good they have done. And all who were saved yet so as by fire, will have received just recompense for the wrongs they have done.

> *He that doeth wrong shall receive for the wrong which he hath done: and there is no respect of persons.*
> (Colossians 3:25)

When the 1000 years are over, all saints will be transferred to the New heaven and the New earth and presented to the Father by Christ, in His righteousness with exceeding joy (Jude 24) and all the tears will be wiped away. (Revelation 21:1-4)

As I see it there is no contradiction. One passage is about the security of the believer being guaranteed by God. The other is about accountability and recompense to all believers for the deeds done in the body. That will happen during the 1000 year reign of Christ on this earth (His kingdom). Some carnal Christians will not get into that kingdom because of their works (1 Corinthians 6:9-20) (Ephesians 5:5) but that will not have any effect on their salvation. That is based on the work that Christ has done. (verses 19-20)

When all accounts have been settled, Christ's reign on this earth ends but the kingdom is transferred to the New Heaven and New Earth and never ends.

> *Then cometh the end when he shall have delivered up the kingdom to God, even the Father; when he shall have put down all rule and all authority and power. For he must reign till he has put all enemies under his feet. The last enemy to be destroyed is death. And when all things shall be subdued unto him, then shall the Son also himself be subject unto him that put all things under him, that God may be all in all. (1 Corinthians 15:24-26, and 28) (Revelation 21:1-4)*

Sixteen reasons not to tell a wayward Christian "He has nothing to Fear"

1 - *Wherefore we labor that whether present or absent, we may be accepted of him, for we must all appear before the judgment seat of Christ; that every one may receive the things done in his body whether good or bad, Knowing therefore the terror of the Lord we persuade men* (2 Corinthians 5: 9 – 11a)

2 - *I keep under my body and bring it into subjection; lest by any means when I have preached unto others I myself should be a castaway* (1 Corinthians 9: 27)

3 - *Vengeance belongeth unto me, I will recompense saith the Lord And again the Lord shall judge his people* (Hebrews 10: 31)

4 - Ananias and his wife were slain by God for their sin and *great fear came upon all the church* (Acts 5: 1 – 11)

5 - *It is a fearful thing to fall into the hands of the living God* (Hebrews 10: 31)

6 - God to Miriam *Wherefore were you not afraid to speak against my servant Moses* (Numbers 12: 8)

7 - *And if ye call on the Father who without respect of persons judgeth according to every man's work, pass the time of your sojourning here in fear* (1 Peter 1: 17)

8 - *For God shall bring every work into judgment with every secret thing whether it be good or whether it be evil* (Ecclesiastes 12: 14)

9 - The judgment may be in this life as with Miriam and Ananias or when He comes to reign (Matthew 24: 51) (Matthew 25: 13 – 30) (Luke 12: 47) *Some men's sins are open beforehand going before to judgment and some they follow after* (1 Timothy 5: 24)

10 - *But he that doeth wrong shall receive for the wrong that he hath done and there's no respect of persons* (Colossians 3: 15)

11 - *That no man go beyond and defraud his brother in any matter for the Lord is the avenger of all such* (1 Thessalonians 4: 6)

12 - *The Lord of that servant shall come in a day when he looketh not for him and in an hour that he is not aware of, and shall cut him asunder and appoint him his portion with the hypocrites. There shall be weeping and gnashing of teeth* (Matthew 24: 50 – 51)

13 - *And cast ye the unprofitable servant into outer darkness; there shall be weeping and gnashing of teeth* (Matthew 25: 30)

14 - *And that servant that knew his Lord's will and prepared not himself neither did according to his will shall be beaten with many stripes* (Luke 12: 47)

15 - If ye do not warn the righteous that turn from their righteousness, his blood will I require at thine hand (Ezekiel 3: 20)

16 - *Is it any wonder that Jesus warned us three times over – Watch therefore for ye know not what hour your Lord doth come – Therefore be ye also ready for in such an hour as ye think not then Son of man cometh*

– *Watch therefore; for ye know neither the day nor the hour when the Son of man cometh* (Matthew 24: 42, 44; and 25: 13)

CHAPTER FIVE

Questions Related To Other Misconceptions About Traditions

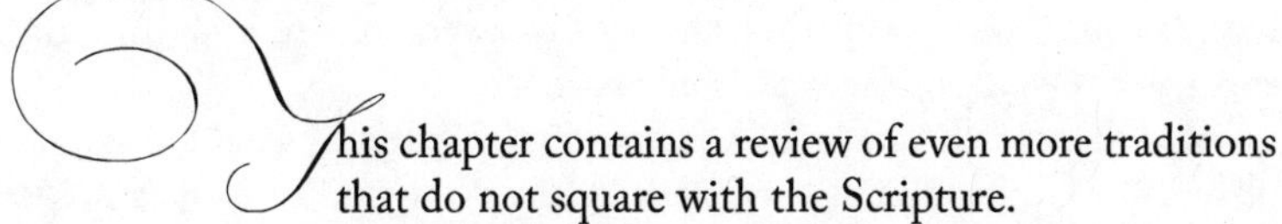

his chapter contains a review of even more traditions that do not square with the Scripture.

Can the saved be lost?

Many knowledgeable Christians believe that this question cannot be answered with a yes or no. I would like to consider the following scriptures on this subject.

> *Who hath also sealed us, and given the earnest [guarantee] of the Spirit in our hearts.* (2 Corinthians 1:22)
>
> *Now he that hath wrought us for the selfsame thing is God, who also hath given unto us the earnest [guarantee] of the Spirit.* (2 Corinthians 5:5)
>
> … *After that ye believed, ye were sealed with that Holy Spirit of promise, which is the earnest [guarantee] of our inheritance until the redemption of the purchased possession, unto the praise of his glory.* (Ephesians 1:13b-14)
>
> *And grieve not the Holy Spirit of God, whereby ye are sealed unto the day of redemption.* (Ephesians 4:30)

In contrast to this we have:

> *But brother goeth to law with brother, and that before the unbelievers. Nay, ye do wrong, and defraud, and that your brethren. Know ye not that the unrighteous shall not inherit the kingdom of God? Be not deceived: neither fornicators, nor idolaters, nor adulterers, nor effeminate, nor abusers of themselves with mankind, nor thieves, nor covetous, nor drunkards, nor revilers, nor extortioners, shall inherit the kingdom of God.* (1 Corinthians 6:6, 8-10)

If inheriting the kingdom of God is the same as being saved, then there is a definite contradiction here. But the term "kingdom of God" does not always mean the same thing – it depends on the context. In

Romans 14:17, the kingdom of God is not meat and drink, but righteousness, peace, and joy in the Holy Ghost. In Luke 8:10-12, it seems to be speaking of salvation. But in Matthew 25:34, He is telling the sheep (Christians) to inherit the kingdom prepared for them from the foundation of the world. They are already saved and are inheriting the earth as a reward for their faithfulness.

This fits with Romans 8:17, where the children of God are said to be heirs of God and joint heirs with Christ if they suffer with Him. As Jesus says in the following:

> *Ye are they which have continued with me in my temptations. And I appoint unto you a kingdom, as my Father hath appointed unto me; that ye may eat and drink at my table in my kingdom, and sit on thrones judging the twelve tribes of Israel.* (Luke 22:28-30)

And consider the following:

> *And whatsoever ye do, do it heartily, as to the Lord, and not unto men; knowing that of the Lord ye shall receive the reward of the inheritance: for ye serve the Lord Christ. But he that doeth wrong shall receive for the wrong which he hath done: and there is no respect of persons.* (Colossians 3:23-25)

The reward of an inheritance in His kingdom will be determined at the judgment seat of Christ (Matthew 19:27-30, Matthew 24:42-51, Matthew 25:1-30, and 2 Corinthians 5:10-11a) when He comes.

> *And, behold, I come quickly; and my reward is with me, to give every man according as his work shall be.* (Revelation 22:12) (Revelation 11:15–18)

> *For the Son of man shall come in the glory of his Father with his angels; and then he shall reward every man according to his works.* (Matthew 16:27)

I believe this is the time when the carnal Christians of 1 Corinthians 6 will discover that they will have no inheritance in that kingdom and will receive for the wrong that they have done (1 Corinthians 3:14-17 and Colossians 3:25). They will suffer the loss of an inheritance in His kingdom, but they shall be saved yet through as by fire.

This is consistent with the entire chapter 6 of 1 Corinthians, right to the last verse, even though he told them in verse 10 that they would not inherit the kingdom. He insists that their bodies and spirits belong to God.

As I see it, there is no contradiction. One passage is about the security of the believer being guaranteed by God. The other is about the accountability of carnality.

To conclude, 2 Peter 1:11 says that His kingdom is an everlasting kingdom that never ends, but the rule of Christ ends after just over 1,000 years. (2 Peter 3:10 and Revelation 20:4-10)

> *For he must reign, till he hath put all enemies under his feet. The last enemy that shall be destroyed is death. And when all things shall be subdued unto him, then shall the Son also himself be subject unto him that put all things under him, that God may be all in all.* (1 Corinthians 15:25, 26, 28)

All accounts will have been settled, including all injustices that Christians have done to each other, and the kingdom, including all the saints, will be transferred to the New Heaven and the New Earth that God will create. (Isaiah 65:17)

The Son will present them to the Father in His righteousness with exceeding joy (Jude 24), and God will wipe away all tears from their eyes (Revelation 21:1-4).

Are wedding garments the same as the "righteousness of Christ"?

No. Wedding garments are not the righteousness of Christ that brings salvation. They are the righteous acts of the saints that qualify them to attend the wedding supper. His wife is arrayed in fine linen, which is the righteous works of the saints. (Revelation 19:8)

> *Let your light so shine before men, that they may see your good works, and glorify your Father which is in heaven.* (Matthew 5:16)

We are exhorted to have our lights burning so as to be ready when the Lord returns from the wedding. (Luke 12:35-36) The reason the Lord did not know them is because they had let their lights go out. (Matthew 25:1-12)

He who says, "I know Him" and does not keep His commandments is a liar. (1 John 2:4)

The Lord has a close relationship with those who keep His commandments, and their wedding garments reflect their obedience. He knows them in a way that He does not know those who are saved, yet so as by fire. (John 14:21-23 and 1 Corinthians 3:15) They are branches in Him who have borne no fruit. They have neglected their responsibility to obey Him – to keep their lights shining. (John 15:1-2) They will not be ready when He comes. (Matthew 25:12-13) Even Paul did not know Him as well as he would have liked. (Philippians 3:10)

Does Matthew 7:13-14 mean that those who take the broad way will go to the lake of fire, and those who take the narrow way are the only ones who will go to heaven?

> *Enter ye in at the straight gate: for wide is the gate, and broad is the way, that leadeth to destruction, and many there be which go in thereat. Because straight is the gate, and narrow is the way, which leadeth unto life, and few there be that find it.* (Matthew 7:13-14)

No. These passages are speaking to Christians about Christians. According to *Strong's Concordance*, destruction means physical, spiritual, or eternal ruin or loss.

Believers are on the broad way that leads to destruction whenever they:

- Are living after the flesh and not after the Spirit (Romans 8:13)
- Walking in darkness (I John 1:6)
- Not abiding in Him (John 15:6)
- Defiling His temple (1 Corinthians 3:16-17)

Christians who are living this way shrivel spiritually and are barren and unfruitful. It was happening in Corinth and it can happen today to any Christian who lets his guard down, neglecting the salvation that God has provided through His Holy Spirit enabling us to walk the narrow way. (1 Corinthians 5:6, 2 Peter 1:8, 10, and Hebrews 2:3) (Romans 8:13, 1 Corinthians 5:6, 2 Peter 1:8-10, Hebrews 2:3) We know one does not have to strive, labour, or work to be saved. Salvation is a gift that we receive by grace through faith, not of works. (Ephesians 2:8-9)

However, we do have to strive to walk the narrow way to an abundant life.

- We are constantly exhorted to: Be sober and vigilant (1 Peter 5:8)
- Do all diligence (2 Peter 1:10)
- Labour to be accepted of Him at the Judgment Seat of Christ (2 Corinthians 5:9-11a). No unbelievers are at this judgment. (Revelations 20:5)

- Exhort one another (Hebrews 10:23-25)
- Put on the armor of God so that we will have a fruitful life (Ephesians 6:11-13)
- Strive for an abundant entrance into the 1,000-year kingdom of our Lord (2 Peter 1:10-11)

We inherit eternal life by faith in what He has done for us. Our inheritance in His 1,000-year kingdom depends on what we have done for Him (Colossians 3:23 – 25).

Is the "rest" we read of in the book of Hebrews a spiritual rest?

Yes, but it is not "only" a spiritual rest. It is also a "literal" rest. Rest is spoken of eleven times in the book of Hebrews. It is the Lord's 1,000-year kingdom when His will is done on earth as it is in Heaven. When Jesus spoke of His kingdom, He nearly always called it the Kingdom of Heaven, and sometimes the Kingdom of God – a time when the whole world will be at rest. (Matthew 6:10)

Jesus said to the disciples:

> *And I appoint unto you a kingdom, as my Father has appointed unto me; that ye may eat and drink at my table in my kingdom, and sit on thrones judging the 12 tribes of Israel.* (Luke 22:29-30)

All the children of God are heirs of God and joint heirs with Christ. (Romans 8:16-17) They will inherit that kingdom with Him if they suffer with Him as the disciples did (Matthew 19:27-30), and do not disqualify themselves as those spoken of in 1 Corinthians 3:16-17, 6:8-10, and Ephesians 5:5. Thousands of Israelites who "fell away" were disqualified from entering the promised land (their rest) but were not disqualified from being the people of God (1 Corinthians 10:1-12). Others who fell included 603,548 men of war who rebelled at Kadesh (Numbers 14:29-30). Numbers 1:1 to 46 lists the total number of men of war as 603,550. All but two died prematurely and did not enter the Promised Land (Joshua 5:4-6) Likewise, Aaron was not allowed to enter the Promised Land (Numbers 20:12 and 24). Neither was Moses for his rebellion. He was not allowed to cross over Jordan. (Numbers 27:12-14)

Therefore, God's children today who "fall away" and disqualify themselves will not be allowed an inheritance in His kingdom. They will be saved as by fire, but they will not enter into His rest. (Ephesians

5:5, 1 Corinthians 3:15, 1 Corinthians 6:6-10) The author of Hebrews pleads, warns, and exhorts us to labour to enter that rest. (Hebrews 3:8, 12-14, 4:1, 4:11, 6:4-6, 12, 10:23-31, 35, 12:15-17)

In conclusion, all believers will go to the New Heaven and the New Earth because of what Christ has done for them. Their inheritance (rest) in His Kingdom depends on what they have done for Him.

How old was Jacob when he incurred the wrath of Esau and fled from Beersheba to Haran? (Genesis 28:10)

The Sons of Jacob (Genesis 35:22-26)

Age of Jacob	Leah	Zilpah	Rachel	Bilhah
77 Came to Haran				
84 - Married				
85	Reuben			
86	Simeon			
87	Levi			
88	Judah			
89		Gad		Dan
90		Ashur		Naphtali
91	Issachar		Joseph	
92	Zebulon			
93	Dinah			
109 - estimate			Benjamin	
147 - Died				

Issachar and Joseph were born on the same year. (Genesis 30:14-26)

Jacob was 77 years of age.

Joseph was 30 years old when he became ruler of Egypt. After seven years of plenty (Genesis 41:53-54), and two years of famine, Joseph would have been 39 (Genesis 45:4-11). Jacob came to Egypt at that time, and his age was 130 years old. (Genesis 47:8-9) From this we know that Joseph was born when Jacob was 91. (Genesis 37:3) When Joseph was born, Jacob had been working for Laban for 14 years (Genesis 30:25-26, 31:41). Genesis 29:14 states that he started working for Laban about one month after they met. Now we know that Jacob left Beersheba just over 14 years before he was 91, so he would have been close to 77 years old when he fled from Beersheba to Haran.

It is interesting to note that Jacob's father Isaac was married at age 40. (Genesis 25:20) His brother Esau was also married at age 40. (Genesis 26:34) Jacob was well past middle age when he married at age 84.

Does God want the relationship between men and women in the church to reflect the order of creation by an outward expression that will vary according to different cultures? Is a woman's hair considered to be her covering?

According to (1 Corinthians 11:1–16), Paul does not base any of his claims on anyone's culture. He disclaims any influence of custom and insists that what he has written in this epistle are the commandments of the Lord. (1 Corinthians 14:37)

The custom of men covering their heads may be a carryover from the laws of the Aaronic priesthood when the priests had to wear bonnets. (Exodus 28:40 and Exodus 29:9)

1 Corinthians 11:1–16 is not about husbands and wives, but about the conduct of men and women in the church. The Hebrew language does not have one word for man and another word for husband, nor do they have one word for woman and another word for wife. It is the same with the Greek language. The context in which the words are used is the only way of determining what is meant. There are two kinds of coverings found in this passage: one artificial and one natural.

"Covering" in verse 4 is *kata* (Greek), obviously an artificial covering for men. In verse 5, "uncovered" (*akatakaluptos*, a variation of *kata*) means a covering for women. "Covered" in verse 6 (*katakalupto*, a variation of *kata*) means a covering for women. "Cover" in verse 7 (*katakalupto*) is the same word with reference to men.

As we know by our nature, long hair is a glory to a woman and long hair is a shame to a man (verse 14).

In verse 15, "covering" (*peribolaion*) is a totally different word that, to my mind, is obviously a natural covering that God has given to a woman to be a glory to her. She is to cover this glory when she prays or prophesies in the church to show her acceptance of the role God planned for women since creation. ("Prophesy" is defined in 1 Corinthians 14:3.) In western countries especially, head coverings for women degenerated into hats designed not to cover their glory, but to accentuate it. This makes the woman's escort the proudest fellow in the Easter parade!

Are those who reject Christ the only ones who the Bible calls hypocrites?

No. Jesus speaks of a servant who was not expecting his lord to come and began to smite his fellow servants and to eat and drink with the drunken. The lord of that servant appointed him his portion with the hypocrites where there shall be weeping and gnashing of teeth. (Matthew 24:48-51)

The purpose of the Judgment Seat of Christ is not to determine who is saved, but to determine what those who are saved will receive for the deeds done in the body after they were saved, whether good or bad. (2 Corinthians 5:10-11a, Matthew 24:42-51, Matthew 25:1-30) The judgment takes place at the beginning of the 1,000 years when Christ has returned and is seated on the throne of His glory. (Matthew 19:27-30 and Revelation 22:12)

Revelation 20:4 indicates that all believers of all ages who have died are said to be in the "first" resurrection and will come with Him when He comes. (1 Thessalonians 3:13 and Zechariah 12:5) The rest of the dead are not resurrected until the 1,000 years are ended, and so we conclude that there cannot be any unbelievers at the Judgment Seat of Christ. (Revelation 20:5) Therefore, the servant who knew his lord's will and did not do it has to be what the Bible calls "carnal" – a servant, but also a hypocrite. (Matthew 24:51 and 1 Corinthians 3:1-3)

In conclusion, believers who are hypocrites will be punished according to their works. No one will be sent to the Lake of Fire to be tormented day and night forever and ever because they were carnal – guilty of envy and strife (1 Corinthians 3:1-3) or a fornicator, covetous, a railer, or a drunkard. (Compare 1 Corinthians 5:11 and 6:18-20.) But, they will be punished according to their works. It is a serious thing to trample underfoot the Son of God and to count the blood of the covenant wherewith one is sanctified an unholy thing and to do despite to the Spirit of grace. (Hebrews 10:26-31) Only those who have rejected the Son who gave His life so that repentant sinners could have their sins forgiven (Luke 24:46-47 and John 3:36) will deserve to go to the place prepared for the devil and his angels.

How do you respond to this question: "What shall they do which are baptized for the dead, if the dead rise not at all?" (1 Corinthians 15:29)

We do not find any instructions or examples in any of the gospels or the epistles indicating that this was taught or practiced by Christ or any of His apostles.

The whole chapter of 1 Corinthians 15 is a discourse on the importance of the resurrection. Water baptism is a confession of faith in what Christ has done. By water baptism, believers are verbally and symbolically saying that Christ died for their sins, that He was buried, and that He rose again for their justification. (Acts 8:35-39, 1 Corinthians 15:3-4, and Romans 4:5)

1 Corinthians 15:29 seems to be saying that if Christ did not rise, water baptism does not make any sense. Why would anyone be baptized to symbolize their faith in Christ's resurrection if he was still in the grave? That would be like being baptized for the dead. 1 Corinthians 15:30-32 continues the same line of thinking when Paul says, "And why stand we in jeopardy every hour? If after the manner of men I have fought with beasts at Ephesus, what advantageth it me, if the dead rise not?"

Baptism has no significance if the dead rise not.

How do you understand "eating His flesh" and "drinking His blood"? (John 6:51–56)

Authors often present the same truths in different ways. I think that a comparison of the things John says on this subject will help us to understand what is meant.

John 1:1, 2 and 14 establishes that the Word was God and that He became flesh.

> *Whoso eateth my flesh, and drinketh my blood, hath eternal life; and I will raise him up at the last day.* (John 6:54)

> *... He that heareth my word, and believeth on him that sent me, has everlasting life ...* (John 5:24)

> *He that eateth my flesh, and drinketh my blood, dwelleth in me, and I in him.* (John 6:56)

An even more intimate relationship is spoken about in John 14:23: "... If a man love me, he will keep my words: and my Father will love him, and we will come unto him, and make our abode with Him."

> *... The words that I speak unto you, they are spirit and they are life.* (John 6:63b)

> *Thy words were found, and I did eat them; and thy word was unto me the joy and rejoicing of my heart ...* (Jeremiah 15:16)

In conclusion, hearing His word and believing in Him is the same as eating His flesh and drinking His blood. Those who have eternal life because they heard His word and believed in Him ate His flesh and drank His blood. They are told to eat the bread and drink the cup that symbolized the broken body and shed blood as a way of remembering the Lord's death until He comes. (1 Corinthians 11:26)

Does Revelation 21:1 mean there will be no sea on the New Earth?

> *And I saw a new heaven and a new earth: for the first heaven and the first earth were passed away; and there was no more sea.* (Revelation 21:1)

I do not think so. The context of the phrase "no more sea" is about the first heaven and the first earth when they pass away with fervent heat; heat that can burn rocks and dust as it did for Elijah on Mount Carmel. Heat so intense that it is hot enough to burn the mountain ranges, will surely vaporize the oceans so that there will be no more sea where the first heaven and the first earth were.

> *But the day of the Lord will come as a thief in the night; in which the heavens shall pass away with a great noise, and the elements shall melt with fervent heat, the earth also and the works that are therein shall be burned up. Nevertheless we, according to his promise, look for new heavens and a new earth, wherein dwelleth righteousness.* (2 Peter 3:10, 13)

Does Revelation 10:5 and 6 mean that time will cease on the New Heaven and the New Earth as implied by the hymn writer?

And the angel ... sware by him that liveth forever and ever ... that there should be time no longer. (Revelation 10:5-6)

No. In view of the context of Revelation 10 and 11, I believe that the phrase "time no longer" means that the 42 months of power given to the beast to make war with the saints and overcome them (Revelation 13:5-7) have ended. From that point, God begins to fulfill the promise made to those saints in Revelation 6:10-11, avenging their blood on those who dwell on the earth. Revelation 9 is a sample of that vengeance.

Revelation 22:2 speaks of the New Heaven and the New Earth, saying: "In the midst of the street of it, and on either side of the river, was there the tree of life, which bare twelve manner of fruits, and yielded her fruit every month."The reference to "month" suggests there will still be time on the New Earth.

What happens to the 5 Virgins of (Mt 25:11-13)

They were carnal Christians who had let their lights go out just as the carnal Christians of (1 Corinthians 6:6–8) were doing, instead of letting their lights shine as in (Mt 5:16) Jesus does not know them in the same way as He knows those who keep his commandments (John 14:21–23). They are not lost, their salvation is guaranteed (Eph 1:13–14) Their bodies are the temple of the Holy Ghost, (1 Co 6:15, 19–20) but they will not have an inheritance in Jesus kingdom (1 Co 6:9–10) (Ephesians 5:5) He did not know them in the sense that they were not abiding in Him (John15: 4) by keeping His commandments

Two Gospels

The word Gospel means good news;

There is the **Gospel of Salvation** as found in (Mark 16: 15 – 16) Go ye into all the world and preach the gospel to every creature. *He that believeth and is baptized shall be saved but he that believeth not shall be damned.*

This is good news to people that realize that; *they are dead in trespasses and sins, having no hope and without God in the world* (Eph 2:1 and 12)

That Gospel is confirmed in many places in different ways such as: (1 Co 15: I – 4) Which says in part, *I declare unto you the gospel which I preached unto you, which you received and by which you are saved. That Christ died for our sins according to the scriptures and that he was buried and that He rose again the third day according to the scriptures.*

The Gospel of salvation also has a down side, which is: He that believeth not shall be damned (Mark 16:16), and again in (John 3:36) - *He that believeth on the Son has everlasting life; and he that believeth not the Son shall not see life; but the wrath of God abideth on him.*

The other Gospel is called **the Gospel of the Kingdom** We read about it in (Matthew 4:23) Which says - *And Jesus went about all Galilee teaching in their synagogues preaching the gospel of the kingdom.* It is a message of good news and hope to those who are born again (John 3:3) and are enduring the trials and tribulations of life and even persecution as in (Matthew 5:10 – 12) Which says in part – *Blessed are they which are persecuted for righteousness sake* (keeping the law and the prophets) (Mathew 7:12) — *Rejoice and be exceeding glad for great is your reward in heaven.*

What does He mean by "reward in heaven?" He makes many references to the kingdom of heaven throughout the Beatitudes of Matthew 4; 5; 6; and 7; When Jesus spoke of "heaven" "kingdom of heaven" "kingdom of God" "kingdom of Christ and of God" "my kingdom" (Luke 22:28 - 30) He was speaking of the time when the beast and the false prophet are cast alive into the lake of fire and Satan is chained in the bottomless pit (Revelation 19:19 – 21) (Revelation 20:1 – 3) and the kingdoms of this world are become the kingdoms of our Lord and of His Christ (Revelation 11:15) and Christ is king over the whole earth (Zechariah 14:9), for 1000 years (Revelation 20:4)

That is when His will, will be done on earth as it is done in heaven, the kingdom he taught them to pray for (Matthew 6:10) That will be the time of reward for all the prophets and saints that have ever lived (Revelation 11:18) (Hebrews 11:36 - 40) It is also the time when the curse of (Genesis 3;) is removed. No more thorns and thistles, no more war, The cow and the bear shall feed and their young ones shall lie down together and the earth shall be full of the knowledge of the Lord as the waters cover the sea (Isaiah 11;) Just as the Gospel of salvation has a downside, so the Gospel of the kingdom also has a downside.

One can be born again and can never lose his salvation and yet not qualify to have any inheritance in the kingdom of heaven (Jesus Kingdom) An inheritance in that kingdom depends on the deeds done in the body. Some people in the church in Corinth (1 Corinthians 6:1 – 20), even though they were bought with a price and their body and spirit belonged to God, they chose to live after the flesh and not after the Spirit, and they will not inherit the kingdom of God, (verses 9,10)

(Ephesians 5:5) says - *For this we know that no whoremonger or covetous man, who is an idolator, hath any inheritance in the kingdom of Christ and of God.*

(1 Corinthians 3:15 – 17) *If any man's work shall be burned he shall suffer loss yet he himself shall be saved ; yet so as by fire. Do ye not know that ye are the temple of God and that the Spirit of God dwelleth in you? If any man defile the temple of God, him shall God destroy (punish), for the temple of God is holy which temple ye are.*

(Matthew 24:49 – 51)(Matthew 25:1 – 13)(Matthew 25:24 - 30) are examples of what it could mean to be destroyed, and why Paul spoke of such judgment as the terror of the Lord (2 Corinthians 5:11a) and why he labored to be accepted of Him - (2 Corinthians 5:9)and not to be a castaway - (1 Corinthians 9: 27) He was not afraid of losing his salvation - (2 Corinthians 5:5 – 6) but he did not want to experience the terror of the Lord, or of outer darkness, or be beaten with many stripes - (Luke 12:47)

Understanding the difference between the Gospel of salvation ,and the Gospel of the kingdom, solves the confusion of whether a saved person can be lost. One's salvation is guaranteed, it cannot be lost (Ephesians 1:13 - 14), But he can lose his inheritance in Jesus Kingdom (1 Co 6:9 - 10) (Ephesians 5:5) and those who do not warn him will be accountable (Ezekiel 3:20)

Conclusion - Our salvation is based on what Jesus has done for us. An inheritance in Jesus millennial kingdom, is based on what we have done for Him.

The Gospel of the Kingdom Oct 11 2016

What is the "Kingdom?" - It is *the kingdom of* (Luke 22:28-30) where Jesus said to his disciples, *You have followed me in my temptations and I appoint unto you a kingdom as my Father has appointed me. That you may eat and drink with me at my table in my kingdom, and rule over the twelve tribes of Israel.* The kingdom of, (Matthew 6:10) - *Thy kingdom come, thy will be done on earth as it is done in heaven.* The kingdom of (Zechariah 14:9) *The Lord shall be king over all the earth in that day.*

How and when will that kingdom come? - In the last days of the tribulation, The kings of the earth will come against the armies of heaven at Armageddon - (Revelation 19:19) The armies of Gog, Persia, Ethiopia, Libya, Gomer and Togarmah, will come against Israel, as a cloud to cover the land - (Ezekiel 38:2, 5, 16) Half of Jerusalem will be taken and the houses rifled and the women ravished - (Zechariah 14:2) Then the fury of God will come up in His face - (Ezekiel 38:18 -23). Jesus will come to the clouds with power and great glory, and all the saints with Him, and every eye shall see him. And when his feet stand on the Mount of Olives there will be the greatest earthquake since man was upon the earth. The powers of heaven shall be shaken, and the stars will fall as figs fall from the tree in a mighty wind. There will be such a shaking of the earth, that it will reel to and fro like a drunkard. Mountains will crumble and walls will tumble. The Mount of Olives will split in half making a great valley. There will be overflowing rain, and 100 pound hailstones, fire and brimstone and pestilence, and a plague, that will cause men's flesh to consume away while they stand on their feet. Their eyes will consume away in their holes and their tongues will consume away in their mouths, and every man's sword will be against his brother. All the fowls of heaven will be called to feast on the dead bodies. (Isaiah 24:20-23) (Ezekiel 38) (Zechariah 14:1-9) (Matthew 24:29 -50) (Revelation 1:7 ; 6:13 ; 16:16 ; 19:20 ; 20:1-3) (Hebrews 12:26)

At Armageddon, the beast and false prophet are cast alive into the lake of fire - (Re 19:20:) and Satan chained in the bottomless pit for a 1000 years - (Revelation 20:1-7

And at that time, *The kingdoms of this world will be the kingdoms of our Lord and of his Christ* - (Revelation 11:15) We call it the second coming of Christ. Jesus called it His kingdom - (Luke 22:30). Peter calls it: *The restitutuon of all things which God hath spoken of by the mouth of all his holy prophets since the world began* - (Acts 3:21) It is the time of the Judgment Seat of Christ, when Jesus will decide what every saint will get for the deeds done in the body, whether good or bad - (2 Corinthians 5:10 -11 a) (Revelation 11:18)

Isaiah, and Ezekiel, Daniel and Zechariah wrote whole chapters about that kingdom. The disciples argued about who would be greatest - (Luke 22:24) The Mother of James and John asked if her sons could sit on either side of Him in his kingdom - (Matthew 20:20-21) Jesus, Peter, John & Paul, exhort us constantly, to be ready for that kingdom. Even the thief knew about it, saying - *Lord remember me when you come into your kingdom* - (Luke 23:42) (Titus 3:8)

Jesus talked more about that kingdom than any other topic. He called it Heaven, or the kingdom of heaven, or the kingdom of God, over 120 times. He talked to his disciples about it, right up to the moment he ascended to heaven - (Acts 1:3-6). He was so enthused at the prospect of rewarding all the prophets, and saints, for what they endured for him, (Hebrews 11:36-40) (Revelation 20:4-5) (Revelation 11:18) That he went about all Galilee, teaching in the villages, and cities, and in their synagogues, the "Gospel" of the Kingdom - (Matthew 4:23) (9-35)

What is that "Gospel?" It is the promise of reward, at the resurrection of the "Just"

Three examples of that gospel are as follows:

Example # One - (Luke 14:13-14) *When you make a feast, call the poor, the maimed, the lame the blind and you shall be <u>blessed</u>. for they cannot recompence you : for you shall be <u>recompenced</u> at the resurrection of the Just.* (Revelation 20:4-6)

This gospel has two parts - "Blessing" and "Reward." The **Blessing**, the *first part,* is Spiritual. It is an inexplicable inner sense of righteousness and peace and joy that comes from the kingdom of God that is in us - (Luke 17:21). Also (Romans 14:17) which says - *The kingdom of God is not meat and drink but righteousness, peace and joy in the Holy Ghost.* People that do good for the Lord's sake can relate to that.

Example # two - (Matthew 5:11-12) - *Blessed are you when men revile you and persecute you and say all manner of evil against you falsely for my sake. Rejoice and be exceeding glad, for great is your reward in heaven.* That is not so easy to relate to.

How can people rejoice when they are being persecuted? It is totally unnatural, but it happened to Paul and Silas. At Phillippi they were preaching the Gospel of Salvation and the magistrates rent off their clothes and had them beaten with many stripes, and put in prison with their feet fast in the stocks. Yet at midnight, they were so overwhelmed with such a sense of righteousness and peace and joy from the Holy Spirit within them, that they began praying and singing praises to God - (Acts 16:19-25) That would be the "**Blessing**." An inner sense the peace of God, that passes all understanding, (Philippians 4:7)

The *second* part, "**Reward**" is "Literal." It is called recompence in (Luke 14: 14) *Thou shalt be recompenced at the resurrection of the Just.* It does not come in this life, It comes when the first resurrection is completed and every saint that has died since creation, has been resurrected. (Revelation 20:4-6) - says in part - *And I saw the souls of them that were beheaded for the witness of Jesus and had not worshipped the beast or received his mark, and they lived - (were resurrected) and reigned with Christ a* **thousand years.** *But the rest of the dead lived not again till the thousand years are finished. This is the first resurrection. Blessed and holy is he that hath part in the first resurrection. On such the second death hath no power.*

Throughout the book of Hebrews, that 1000 year period is called a "rest" for the people of God (Hebrews 3:8-19; 4:1-11). It is the literal part of the gospel of the kingdom. All the people of God come with Jesus, when he comes for his kingdom - (Zechariah 14:5-9) (1 Thessalonians 3:13) (Revelation 11:15, 18) (Hebrews 11:35-40) (Matthew 16:27) (Revelation 22:12)

Example # Three - (Luke 6:38) - which says in part - *Give - and it shall be given unto you. Good measure — Pressed down — Shaken together — and — Running over.*

Many understand this verse to mean that whatever we give to God, he will give us abundantly more during our lifetime. We know that did not happen to the prophets and saints of (Hebrews 11:39) or to John the baptist or Stephen or any of the apostles. However, if it does'nt mean that what does it mean ? The scriptures we have looked at, clearly teach, that the "Blessing" comes at the time a good deed is done, but the "Reward" does not come until the resurrection of the Just (Luke 14:14), when Jesus comes for His kingdom - (Matthew 19:27:30) (Matthew 16:27) (Revelation 22:12)

To be consistant with the scriptures, we must understand (Luke 6:38) to mean that Those who Give their All to God, will be Blessed, and at the resurrection of the Just, will be given a hundredfold - for 1000 years - (Revelation 20:2, 3, 4, 5, 6, 7)

Good measure - Pressed - down - Shaken together - and - Running over

EPILOGUE

The Prophets, and Jesus, and Peter, and John, and Paul, warned the people of God repeatedly to be ready for His coming and the ensuing Judgment, when all saints will receive for the deeds done in the body, whether good or bad: The time of that Judgment will be when Jesus returns to this earth to receive His kingdom and is seated on the throne of His glory (Matthew 19: 28).

God has given us four basic incentives to motivate believers to be ready for that day :

- Love
  (2 Corinthians 5:14, John 14:2, 1 John 4:10, Hebrews 12:2)
- Reward
  (Matthew 5:11–12, Matthew 16:27, Revelation 11:18)
- Duty
  (1 Corinthians 9:17, 1 John 3:23, Romans 12:1)
- Fear
  (1 Corinthians 9:16, Matthew 24:50–51, Matthew 25:24–30, Colossians 3:25, Acts 5:10 – 11, 2 Corinthians 5:9 11a, Deuteronomy 17:12-13, Hebrews 10:29)

All of these incentives work together to motivate believers to make the right choices in life, and be "ready" when He comes. Even Paul labored to be "ready" for that judgment. (2 Corinthians 5:9-11a)

It is so easy to deceive one's self - this author thought he loved the Lord, until the Lord drew his attention to (John 14:15), "If ye love me, keep my commandments", and (1 Peter 2:13), "Submit yourselves to every ordinance of man for the Lord's sake".

It was then, he realized that he did not even love the Lord enough to "forsake" the pleasure of speeding, “for the Lord's sake". The conviction of his sin, and the " fear " of receiving for the bad he was doing, led him to repentance, and a change of behavior, resulting in the forgiveness of (Isaiah 55:7) and (1 John 1:9) Many Bible expositors today, seem determined to eliminate the God-given "fear factor" of (Deuteronomy 17:12-13), (Numbers 12:8-10), (Acts 5:10–11), (2 Corinthians 5:11a), (Hebrews 10:28–31), (1 Peter 1: 17–19), as an incentive for obedience, by wresting the Holy scriptures, to make them conform to a false tradition (2 Peter 3:16) and taking (Romans 8:1) completely out of its context, and teaching that there is no condemnation (punishment) for a Christian, regardless of how he lives, (see pages 31, 70, 72 and 73) and saying:

- A bad work is not a moral wrong
- Fear does not mean to be afraid
- Terror does not mean frighten
- Bema, a Greek word, does not mean judgment seat

Surely, the time to search the Scriptures to see if these things are so is long overdue.

Printed in Canada